DISABILITY
DISCRIMINATION

DISABILITY
DISCRIMINATION

A Practical Guide to the New Law

Second Edition

JEAN BRADING and JOHN CURTIS

KOGAN
PAGE

First published in 1996
Second edition in 2000

Kogan Page Limited
120 Pentonville Road
London N1 9JN

British Library Cataloguing in Publication Data

A CIP record for this book is available from the British Library.

ISBN 0 7494 2778 7

Typeset by Florence Production Ltd, Stoodleigh, Devon

Printed and bound in Great Britain by
Creative Print and Design, (Wales)

Contents

About the authors   9

Acknowledgements   10

Preface to the second edition   11

The Disability Discrimination Act 1995: a summary   12

Who is affected, and how   12
What the Act does – an outline   13

1. Introduction   15

Background: disability and the law   15
What does this mean for managers?   16
How to use this book   17
Looking to the future   17

PART 1   A PRACTICAL GUIDE TO EMPLOYMENT
          AND DISABILITY

2. Work today: diversity and opportunity   21

Current trends   21
What does disability really mean?   24
What sort of disabilities are you likely to encounter
  at work?   26
Different disabilities and their implications   26
Moving towards equality   31
An example of equal opportunities initiatives   37

3. Communication and disability — 41

Setting the scene — 41
Three approaches to disability — 42
Taking down the barriers: disability awareness
    training — 43
Dealing with resistance: 360° commitment — 46
What price political correctness? — 48
Preferred language — 48
Some tips on meeting someone with a disability — 49
The competent manager of disabled people — 50

4. Employing disabled people — 52

Being fair: recruitment and selection — 52
What happens in practice? — 60
Psychometric testing — 62
Assessment and development centres (AC/DC) — 65
Access: enabling people to participate — 67
Interviews — 68
Welcoming someone with a disability into your team — 70
Career development — 72
Sickness absence — 73
Retention: employees who become disabled — 75
Selection for redundancy — 78
Health and safety — 79
Dismissal — 80
Proactive disability management at work — 82
Insurance matters — 83
A note on costs — 84
Some more ideas . . . — 85
Seeking advice from outside — 86
Keeping up the good work: monitoring progress — 87

5. Policies and codes — 88

Putting it all into practice: plans for action — 88
The national approach: suggestions from the Government — 88
The Employers' Forum on Disability — 90
Local policy and practice networks — 92
Policy statements — 92
Equal opportunities within a wider context — 95
An example of an effective code of practice — 95

6. **Sources of support**   **108**

   Statutory help   109
   Voluntary sector help   113
   Employer networks   114
   Schemes and initiatives   114
   Disability consulting groups   118
   ACDET (Advisory Committee for Disabled People in
      Employment and Training)   118

PART 2   LEGISLATIVE CHANGES

7. **Employment provisions of the DDA**   **121**

   Introduction   121
   The detailed requirements   122
   Disability definition   122
   Discrimination by employers   129
   Dismissal – and links with earlier legislation   130
   Making reasonable changes – duty of an employer to
      make adjustments   134
   Complaints   141
   Questionnaire procedure   142
   Victimization   147
   Likely impact of the DDA   147

8. **Other areas covered by the Act**   **149**

   Goods, facilities, services and premises   149
   Education   150
   Transport   152
   The National Disability Council   152
   Disability Rights Commission Act 1999   152
   The Disability Rights Task Force   153

Postscript   Disability: some further issues   **155**

Appendix 1.   List of common conditions   **156**

Appendix 2.   The statute   **161**
   Disability Rights Commission Act 1999   161

Appendix 3.   Providing access for all   **196**
   Building specifications   196
   Assessing the accessibility of venues   200

Appendix 4.   Useful names and addresses   **203**
  Local employer networks on disability   212

Bibliography   **213**

Index   **215**

About the authors

Jean Brading has a background in human resources management (HRM) and consultancy, specializing in disability and diversity issues. She has published widely in professional journals and other media. Jean has a BA in English, a Diploma in Personnel Management, and certificates in counselling, training and psychometric testing. She is a Member of the Institute of Personnel and Development and the Institute of Careers Guidance. At the time of writing she is completing an MSc at Birkbeck College in Organizational Behaviour, and is a visiting fellow at City University.

John Curtis was formerly Director of Skill: National Bureau for Students with Disabilities, and earlier in the Department of Employment, where he specialized in the management of services for people with disabilities. He is an MPhil of the University of Sussex, an associate member of the Institutes of Personnel and Development and Careers Guidance, a Fellow of the Royal Society of Arts, and a visiting fellow of City University.

Charterhouse Partnership has been formed by Jean and John in response to the demand from employers for guidance on working with disability issues, and on implementing the provisions of the Disability Discrimination Act. Charterhouse also compiles expert witness employment reports for the courts in cases of discrimination and personal injury compensation claims.

Charterhouse Partnership, Birchland, Ravensworth Road,
Mortimer West End, Reading RG7 3UD
Telephone: 0118 333 3366; Fax: 0118 933 3662;
e-mail: mail@charterhouse-partnership.co.uk;
Web site: www.charterhouse-partnership.co.uk

Acknowledgements

We are grateful to the many friends and colleagues who supported us in the writing of this book, and who readily contributed to discussions about its contents.

Particular thanks are due to Mike Brading, for all his practical suggestions and invaluable technological help. We should also like to thank Sylvia Curtis, and Claire, Anna and Sarah Brading, for putting up with more neglect than usual, and for encouraging us in this work.

Jean Brading and John Curtis

Preface to the second edition

Although this book was first published in May 1996, the employment provisions it describes only came into effect as of 2 December 1996. This second edition enables us to report what has happened since then, in particular some of the tribunal and employment appeal tribunal decisions which help to interpret the original legislation. We are indebted to Gary Bowker, one of the editors of *Equal Opportunities Review*, for tribunal case-study material and to Paul Brown, barrister, for providing other material and information.

The latest development is the passing of the Disability Rights Commission Act 1999 and the beginning of the Commission's activity in April 2000. We have given brief details at the end of the book and the whole statute is reproduced in Appendix 2.

Jean Brading and John Curtis
May 2000

The Disability Discrimination Act 1995: a summary

WHO IS AFFECTED, AND HOW

- *Disabled people* who have a physical, mental or sensory disability, which is substantial and long term (12 months) and which makes it difficult for them to carry out normal day-to-day activities, have new rights of non-discrimination.
- *Employers of 15 or more people* now act unlawfully if they discriminate against current or prospective employees because of their disability, unless there is a good reason.
- *Providers of services* have to take reasonable measures to ensure that they do not discriminate against disabled people.
- *Landlords and others who are responsible for letting, selling or managing property* need to ensure that they do not unreasonably discriminate against disabled people.
- *Schools, colleges and universities* are required to supply information about their provision for disabled pupils and students.

Some people obviously have to take action under two or more of the above measures.

WHAT THE ACT DOES – AN OUTLINE

The Disability Discrimination Act 1995

The Disability Discrimination Act introduced provisions aimed at tackling the discrimination that many disabled people face. The Act gives disabled people new rights in the areas of:

- employment;
- access to goods, facilities and services;
- buying or renting land or property.

On 2 December 1996, all the main duties on employers came into force, including all duties to make 'reasonable adjustments'. At the same time some initial duties on providers of goods, facilities and services and on trade organizations came into force, though not duties to make 'reasonable adjustments'. Duties in relation to the buying or renting of land or property also came into force at this time.

From 1 October 1999, new duties were placed on service providers to make 'reasonable adjustments' for disabled people, such as providing extra help or making changes to the way they provide their services. It is intended that, from 2004, service providers will also have to make 'reasonable adjustments' to the physical features of their premises to overcome physical barriers to access. The duties on trade organizations to make reasonable adjustments follow a similar timetable.

There are Codes of Practice to give guidance on these new duties. Separate Codes give guidance for employers and for service providers. There is also published Guidance on matters to be taken into account in determining questions relating to the definition of disability. The Codes and Guidance can be obtained from Stationery Office bookshops – see Bibliography at the back of this book. Advice on which Codes are currently in force, or supplies of free explanatory leaflets, can be obtained by phoning the DRC helpline on 0345 622 633.

In addition, the Act:

- requires schools, colleges and universities to provide information for disabled people;
- allows the Government to set minimum standards so that disabled people can use public transport easily;
- set up the National Disability Council to advise the Government on the elimination of discrimination against disabled people.

In April 2000, a Disability Rights Commission was established with the following duties: to work towards the elimination of discrimination against disabled people, to promote the equalization of opportunities for disabled people, to take such steps as it considers appropriate with a view to encouraging good practice in the treatment of disabled people and to keep under review the working of the Disability Discrimination Act 1995. The National Disability Council ceased to exist when the Disability Rights Commission was set up.

Northern Ireland

The Act also applies in Northern Ireland. A Code of Practice reflecting those certain modifications is published in Northern Ireland.

1

Introduction

BACKGROUND: DISABILITY AND THE LAW

For over 50 years the main, and virtually only, legislation about employing disabled people has been the Disabled Persons (Employment) Act 1944. This Act laid upon employers of 20 or more people a duty to have a percentage of registered disabled people in their workforce. Since it was not an offence to fail in that duty, the requirement could not easily be enforced. Hence disabled people became reluctant to register as disabled so that eventually it could not be enforced at all – there were simply not enough eligible people to meet the quota, which for many years had been 3 per cent.

So after a half century of trying unsuccessfully to legislate for equal opportunity by head counting, the government enacted the Disability Discrimination Act 1995 (DDA). The new Act repealed the registration and quota aspects of the 1944 Act, though existing registered disabled people retained their registration for three years. Instead, it has become unlawful for an employer to discriminate against disabled people in employment, that is, to treat them less favourably than someone else because of their disability, unless there is a good reason. This provision applies to all aspects of employment including recruitment, training, promotion and dismissal. Employers of fewer than 15 people are exempt from the employment part of the Act, though not from its other parts. The employment provisions also do not apply to operational staff in the armed forces, the police, the prison service, fire service, or to anyone employed on board ships, hovercraft or aeroplanes. There are special rules for contract workers.

15

Employers also have a positive duty to make reasonable adjustments to prevent substantial disadvantage to disabled people. These matters are fully dealt with later in the book.

WHAT DOES THIS MEAN FOR MANAGERS?

Unravelling the complexity of the DDA is providing lawyers with many opportunities for discussion and debate. Until we have a good body of case law, there will be much room for interpretation. But what you, as a manager, will want to know is the likely impact of the legislation on your business: or, put another way, how to turn a necessity into an opportunity.

In Chapter 2 we look at the business benefits to be gained from employing a diverse workforce. The irony is that many organizations have in the past remained closed to such strategies, only to find that, for a variety of reasons, they perhaps have not maximized their use of the people available to them.

Why have employers remained so inactive on disability issues?

Employers will not readily admit to being prejudiced about people with disabilities, and some probably are not, but there is much evidence that when experiences of people with disabilities are examined, it becomes clear that most of their problems arise from the attitudes of employers. A general lack of understanding about the employment of people with disabilities gives rise to numerous myths and fears which create prejudice and discrimination – see for example Honey et al (1993).

Many employers fail to appreciate that disability does not necessarily imply inability and a disability may not result in handicap (Kettle, 1979). Many managers therefore assume that people with disabilities would not be able to perform adequately at work. Others have low expectations and think only of lower skilled jobs. Other myths include poor attendance, low productivity, proneness to accidents, customers being put off and disabled workers' presence being disruptive. Kettle argues that the persistence of these misconceptions is not entirely the fault of employers, and blames the medical profession for being over-cautious about the abilities of people with disabilities.

Thomas (1992) found that one of the main reasons for people giving up work was that their GPs had told them they would never work again, and never properly considered the options of retraining and redeployment. If doctors are regarded as the experts in these matters, it is no wonder that any employers' negative feelings are reinforced (Barnes, 1991).

Most discussion about disability takes place in contexts of medicine, sociology and psychology – not areas in which most managers necessarily operate. The main purpose of this book therefore is to bring the issues into the management arena, using the DDA as a vehicle for capturing managers' interest and enthusiasm.

HOW TO USE THIS BOOK

Our aim in writing this book is to demystify, in a readable way, the whole subject of disabled people and employment. For this reason, Chapters 2–6 (Part 1) are written in the spirit of the Act, without referring too much to the detail. These chapters concentrate on good practice and highlight areas for you as a manager to consider in your approach to employing and integrating people with disabilities. Part 1 may therefore be read on its own, in order to gain more understanding of this whole area, and pick up some suggestions on improving relevant management practices. We include employment tribunal decisions to help you relate theory to practice.

If you wish to explore at greater depth the employment provisions of the Act, Chapters 7 and 8 (Part 2) dissect and examine the detailed requirements of the legislation, enabling you to compare your existing procedures with what is needed now that the various parts of the Act have come into force.

LOOKING TO THE FUTURE

No doubt some people will be linking the likely effect of the DDA with what has happened since the race and gender legislation more than 20 years ago. It is a sobering thought that cases are still being fought, and examples brought to light, of inequitable practice in these areas. However, there has certainly been a general improvement in employment terms for these groups of people. Equal opportunities legislation can protect workers and give a stimulus to action to decision-makers within organizations, but more than that, it can pave the way to a more creative organization: one that is responsive to all sections of the market, that values individuality as well as conformity, and that encourages synergy in every aspect of its operations. The influence of Europe, and indeed globalization and legal developments such as the Human Rights Act, which comes into force in October 2000, will all have a major impact on the lives of everyone, and strengthen the case for valuing diversity in practical ways as well as theoretically.

What you want is a motivated, productive, committed workforce. Making provision for all workers so that they may give of their best makes sense. We hope that this book will help you build on the strengths of people with disabilities, to the benefit of both them and your organization.

PART 1

A PRACTICAL GUIDE TO EMPLOYMENT AND DISABILITY

This part of the book aims to present you with current thinking on how to make the most of the contribution offered to you by people with disabilities. It looks at the meaning and impact of disability, how to treat disabled people fairly in all aspects of employment, how to construct a code of practice and statement of equal opportunities, where to get expert help, and how training and involvement can help deal with resistance and prejudice. We believe that if you follow our suggestions, you will find that you are well on the way to complying with the detailed requirements of the Act. However, we are not lawyers by profession, and would urge readers to take legal advice on any specific issues where there is doubt about their procedures or policies.

2

Work today: diversity and opportunity

CURRENT TRENDS

Changes in the working world

The world of work is changing. The beginning of the new century is proving to be a time of increased growth in the economy, while at the same time the nature of jobs is evolving rapidly. E-commerce and the Internet have transformed many sectors of employment.

Manufacturing is declining, to be outstripped by the service sector. Even where traditional manual skills are still used, there is a shift towards the use of information technology as part of a systems approach to work, supplanting routine processes requiring manual dexterity. A different set of skills is needed for the twenty-first century workforce, and many of these skills are related to communication of one sort or another, with flexibility being at a premium.

Employees nowadays have more choices as to how to earn their money. New ways of working can encompass working part time for one or maybe more employers, at the same time as contributing on a voluntary basis in the community. Increases in part-time employment possibilities are good news for many people, enabling them to create the most satisfying balance in their lives. Different experiences also result in the opportunity to amass a range of complementary skills and knowledge, which can then be transferred into other parts of life, whether or not they are fee-paying. Employability, rather than employment, is seen as the key to a successful working life.

As we move into the twenty-first century, many people are finding that, as a result of delayering within organizations, the traditionally structured job holds more responsibility and is more stressful. The syndrome referred to as 'presenteeism', where workers are frightened of redundancy to the point that they work endlessly long hours, has been a real threat to innovation and maximized potential. Employers are consistently seeking ways of improving organizational commitment. Similarly people who are self-employed find that they must be totally dedicated in order to keep their share in the market, since changes happen so quickly now and demand immediate responses.

The impact of technology

Teleworking is increasing in popularity. More and more individuals now work from home (or possibly from a local telecottage) using a mixture of computer, fax and telephone technology. A recent survey by Henley Management College found that 70 per cent of large- and medium-sized businesses plan to introduce some form of remote working over the next two years. From the organization's point of view, introducing teleworking may well cut costs: you don't need as much floor space, for example. Many employees find the thought of avoiding expensive and time-consuming commuting attractive. But there are management issues. The old 'command and control' school of management has no place here. Sir Peter Thompson, former president of the privatized National Freight Consortium, said (at a 1995 conference, held as part of the first European Telework Week) that employers should introduce teleworking only if the organization had a culture of local accountability and trust. However, with multinational organizations working across time zones, e-mail, which can be accessed anywhere in the world at any time, puts new pressures on employees.

Workers themselves are changing

More and more women are entering the world of work, so that by 2001 they will make up over 50 per cent of employees, even though at the moment they are still under-represented in higher level occupations. The workforce is also ageing, as the baby boomers move towards retirement. More people from ethnic minorities are seeking work, and increasing numbers of people now have some sort of qualification. This is seen as a positive step towards the lifelong learning approach which is advocated by the government.

People with disabilities

In total, 6.4 million people (ie 18 per cent of the working-age population) have a work-limiting health problem or disability. In 1998/9, the economic activity rate for disabled people of working age was only 51 per cent compared with 85 per cent for non-disabled people (*Labour Market Trends*, September 1999).

There is no doubt that unemployment has a disproportionate impact on disabled people. They find it more difficult to obtain work, and are more likely to be unemployed for longer. However, the DDA should help to facilitate the entry into and retention in work of disabled people.

Currently people with disabilities are more likely to be in part-time work or self-employment. As mentioned earlier, this tendency does actually mesh with current trends in the labour market in general. However it is also true that disabled people are under-represented in higher level jobs. It is difficult to pinpoint exactly why this should be the case. It may be a reflection of employers' reluctance to risk employing an unknown quantity such as disabled people, particularly if they equate disability with ill health. It may also stem from disabled people's relative inability to access the system: they have perhaps been excluded by barriers which were not relevant to the carrying out of the job in question. *Labour Market Trends* shows that disabled people of working age are less likely to hold educational qualifications than non-disabled people in the same age group (and this can be for a variety of reasons which may have nothing to do with intellectual ability). Certainly the long-term unemployment rates are quite different from one another; see Table 2.1.

Table 2.1 *Unemployed over 1 year, UK, winter 1998/9, not seasonally adjusted*

Age group	Non-disabled (%)	Disabled (%)
16–24	11.5	22.9
25–34	27.6	33.2
35–49	34.0	43.9
50–59/64	46.1	48.6
16–59/64	25.8	38.1

Source: *Labour Market Trends*, September 1999

23

The impact of all these factors . . .

What all this means in practical terms is that there are many disabled people whose skills are under-utilized at present, but for whom the increasingly flexible job market may offer unprecedented opportunities. For employers too this is good news. By following the provisions in the DDA, and by creating more scope for people with disabilities, they will themselves be gaining improved access to a wide range of experienced and skilled individuals. This will enable organizations to match their growth and changing structures more responsively to the available pool of labour, thus maximizing their potential profit.

WHAT DOES DISABILITY REALLY MEAN?

The answer to this question depends very much on your personal involvement in the subject. People who have had no personal contact with people who are disabled tend to think rather simplistically in terms of someone who is a wheelchair user, or who has learning difficulties. Maybe they recall some element of embarrassment or fascination on encountering someone in the street who seemed different from others. Perhaps they are reminded of parental injunctions not to stare, and they avert their eyes.

A large element of this kind of reaction comes as a result of the segregation that exists in our society, where people who are perceived as different tend to be housed and educated behind closed doors, away from all the 'normal' people. The distance implicit in this kind of polarized approach to disability – that person is abnormal and I'm not – is responsible for many of the barriers which we examine in Chapter 3.

For today's organization to make maximum use of all the available resources, human and otherwise, it is important to take a more informed and dispassionate look at what constitutes a disability and what effect the existence of an impairment might have on a person's ability to perform particular tasks.

Defining disability

The first thing to be aware of in defining disability is the tendency to confuse disability with ill health. They are not the same. Disability in many cases is relative: it depends on the environment and on who is doing the defining! We also need to consider whether we are talking in diagnostic terms (the name of the condition) or in functional terms (the effect the disability has on everyday life). Here are three traditionally accepted definitions:

An impairment is any loss or abnormality of psychological, physio-logical or anatomical structure or function. (This is dealing with parts or systems of the body that do not work.)
A disability is any restriction or lack (resulting from an impair-ment) of ability to perform an activity in the manner or in the range considered normal for a human being. (This refers to things people cannot do.)
A handicap is the disadvantage that results from a disability.

These distinctions can seem a bit confusing, so here are some illus-trations to help to clarify them.

Joanne's impairment is brittle bone disease which she has had since birth. Although she has developed many coping strategies and can get around independently using a wheelchair, her inability to walk is a disability. This becomes a handicap if she tries to move around in a building without ramps or lifts. However, the installation of these removes her handicap.

Suresh's health condition is asthma. His disability is the breathlessness caused by lifting, running and climbing stairs. Suresh will find this a handicap if he wants to become a bricklayer.

Annette has experienced epileptic fits since the age of seven. Her health condition is epilepsy. As a result of medication she only experiences fits while asleep and so, providing she takes her medication as prescribed, she does not have any disabilities. However, Annette finds that some people are fearful of her condition and she may be handicapped by their prejudices.

Source: Bosley (1994)

The new definition

The DDA introduces a new core definition of disability:

> Either a physical or mental impairment, which has a substantial and long-term adverse effect on a person's ability to carry out normal day-to-day activities.

This definition has been criticized for not taking into account the effect of other people's perceptions. (For more detail on the defini-tion, see Chapter 7.) In the employment scenario, it is of paramount importance not to let personal prejudices and individual assumptions take the place of a reasoned appraisal of exactly what an individual is capable of: as always, the starting point must be to consult the person with a disability, since he or she is the expert.

WHAT SORT OF DISABILITIES ARE YOU LIKELY TO ENCOUNTER AT WORK?

Any sort! Many disabilities are hidden, and people may choose not to disclose their existence, particularly if there is no benefit to them in doing so.

The likelihood of particular disabilities being made known to you is indicated by the results of a report published in 1993 by the Institute of Employment Studies, entitled *Employers' Attitudes Towards People with Disabilities*. This survey studied contemporary practice in the employment of people with disabilities, through a mixture of a literature search, a postal survey, and a series of in-depth case studies. The report showed that problems associated with walking, climbing stairs and maintaining balance accounted for 40 per cent of economically active people with disabilities. The next most common problems are those to do with hearing (20 per cent), and intellectual functioning (19 per cent). Disabilities related to behaviour, dexterity and vision were also shown to be important.

DIFFERENT DISABILITIES AND THEIR IMPLICATIONS

Providing a list of common disabilities and impairments in a sense goes against the ethos of this book. Our core message to the reader is to consult the individual, since he or she is the person best qualified to advise on working arrangements and capacity. However, we recognize that one of the components of a better appreciation of the elements of disability is confidence, and that may be gained through increased knowledge. For this reason we include here a list of starting points for discussion, for you to explore at greater length with the people with disabilities in your organization.

Physical and motor impairments

Many people with disabilities fall into this category, since it includes both congenital conditions (for example, cerebral palsy) and disabilities which have arisen through accidents.

26

The main implication in terms of your role as manager is ensuring equality of access in the widest possible sense. This may include physical considerations, such as convenient car parking spaces or alterations to buildings, or accommodation for a notetaker or personal assistant. Funding may be available through Access to Work (see Chapter 6).

Back Injury Not Disability

Rowley v Walkers Nonsuch Ltd

As a result of a back injury suffered at work, Mrs Rowley went on sick leave. She had been off work for six months and had submitted a further sick note, certifying her unfit for work for a further 13 weeks, when her employer dismissed her on 13 December 1996 after 22 years' service on grounds that it could not reasonably wait any longer for her to return. It stated the reason to be incapability due to ill health. Dismissing her claim under the DDA, a Shrewsbury industrial tribunal (Chair: S J Williams) found that her condition could not be said, on the evidence, to fall within the definition of disability under the Act.

We do not find it possible to say that she had a physical impairment which had, at that time, a substantial and long-term adverse effect on her ability to carry out normal day-to-day activities. The employers in late 1996 could not predict the future, but at that time we would not say that the condition of which we have heard came within that definition.

23 April 1997; case no. 2900173/97.

Visual impairments

There are about 2 million visually-impaired people in the UK, of whom an estimated 1.5 million are unable to read newsprint.

In the workplace, access to information is the major concern. Not everyone can use Braille, so the best approach is to ask the person what form of assistance would be most appropriate to them. Examples include: a personal reader, Braille, large print or taped materials, and specialist equipment such as speech synthesizers. If the person is accompanied by a guide dog, some provision for exercising the animal will have to be organized. Getting to and from work may also be an issue.

Deaf and hearing-impaired people

Not many people are unable to hear anything at all. But even those who are not completely deaf may experience difficulty in communication. Many people use a mixture of lip reading, a hearing aid, and perhaps sign language. For those who are profoundly deaf, it is important to remember that sign language, as opposed to English, is their first language, and this will have implications in terms of how they fill in application forms and so on.

As a manager of a deaf person, you may find you need to provide equipment such as a minicom (a text telephone), an induction loop (an amplification device which may be either portable or permanently fitted into buildings), or a person to act as communicator, for example a sign language interpreter.

Learning difficulties

Everyone differs in his or her ability to assimilate information and act on it. People who are assessed as markedly different from what is expected of their age group are described as having learning difficulties. In education, they are often classified as having moderate or severe learning difficulties. It is unlikely (though possible) that you will find someone with severe learning difficulties in anything other than supported employment (see Chapter 6).

As the manager of someone with moderate learning difficulties, you will need to ensure that any problems of accessing and understanding information are ironed out. You will need to convey information in simple unambiguous language and be prepared to reinforce it. After training, which might need to be intensive and prolonged, your employee will provide excellent service in any one of a number of routine jobs.

Specific learning difficulties

The most common form of this group of disabilities is dyslexia. It can be found in people throughout the whole ability range. Some might be very gifted in certain areas, while needing help in others.

Accessing the written or printed word is the most usual problem and you and your employee will need to discuss ways of coping. People with dyslexia are often helped at the simplest level by the use of a computer for spell checking. They might also benefit from receiving information on tape or disk rather than in printed form.

Mental health

Stress has been in the news a lot recently, particularly in relation to compensation claims. Everyone has different abilities to deal with stress, and outside influences such as events at home may impact on the work environment. It is possible for employees to go through a period of finding it difficult to cope with everyday life, and yet be able to return to work all the stronger for having coped with such adversity.

Managing someone who encounters a period of mental ill health calls for patience and extra sensitivity and support. You may want to provide the person with counselling, or coaching in time management, or whatever else seems appropriate. If the person is depressed, you may find it difficult to communicate with him or her. Take advice from someone who has dealt with this situation before, and ask the person concerned what their needs are. Mental health problems which occurred in the past are largely covered by the DDA (although there are some exceptions; see Chapter 7). This means your keeping an open mind and taking a positive approach, particularly when reading application forms from people who have, for example, experienced an episode of schizophrenia.

Mental-illness Dismissal Unlawful

Lang v Redland Roofing Systems Ltd

An Edinburgh industrial tribunal (Chair: S F R Patrick) holds that the dismissal of an employee because her medical certificate used the word 'psychosis' in circumstances where she would not have been dismissed if the certificate had given a physical illness as the reason for the absence, was unlawful disability discrimination.

Alison Lang, who has a form of mental illness called 'bi-polar affective disorder', was employed by Redland Roofing Systems Ltd as an internal sales representative from 8 January 1996 until 3 June 1997, when she was dismissed. She was absent from work between 15 May and 16 July, during which time she was admitted for hospital in-patient treatment. A medical certificate showed 'mood disorder' as the cause of absence. There was a change in her behaviour on her return to work and during the subsequent months her performance began to give cause for concern. She was the subject of a number of complaints from customers. In May 1997, following a review, she was informed by her sales manager that he was 'looking for a substantial improvement in her performance' and a formal written warning was issued. Shortly afterwards, Ms Lang was absent from work and

---

submitted a medical certificate giving as the cause of absence 'psychosis', and recorded that she would be off work for a month. Her employer took this to mean that she had a serious mental disorder. On 3 June she was dismissed because of 'inability to carry out the role of internal sales representative due to your continued health problems'. She claimed discrimination under the DDA.

Upholding her claim, the tribunal accepted that at the time of her dismissal she was a disabled person within the meaning of s.1(2) of the DDA. Bi-polar affective disorder is a clinically well-recognized mental illness, said the tribunal. Although the effects of the impairment were alleviated by the medical treatment the applicant was receiving, this was ignored by the tribunal in accordance with para. 1 of Schedule 1 to the Act of para. 11 of annex 1 of the Disability Code of Practice. The impairment is taken to have the effect it would have had without such treatment. It had a substantial and long-term adverse effect on her ability to carry out normal day-to-day activities. It had lasted for 12 months and, according to medical evidence, it was likely to last for a further 12 months, if not for the rest of the applicant's life.

In the tribunal's view, it was 'remarkable' that an employer of the respondents' status should dismiss 'so peremptorily, even in relation to an employee with less than two years' service. Even if the respondents had it in mind that the applicant's prospective further absence meant that she could no longer be employed by them, there was no pressing need for them to deal with the matter instantly, especially when the applicant had been signed off for a month. She had barely started upon her second year's entitlement to sick pay.' In all the circumstances, the tribunal drew the inference that whoever made the decision to dismiss did so 'because the medical certificate used the word "psychosis" which was understood to mean a serious mental illness'. It also drew the inference that the same action would not have been taken had the certificate 'disclosed a physical illness as the reason for the absence'. It awarded compensation of £1,712 (plus interest), including £1,000 for injury to feelings.

Case no. S/40788/97

Speech and language impairments

These are most commonly stammers of some degree of severity. Such impairments may result in a person having difficulty expressing him or herself, or inadequately taking in information from other sources.

In employment, the key issue is to find ways of communicating with the person. Sometimes anxiety can exacerbate the impairment, so any means of reducing this is to be explored. Otherwise it may be worth looking at other forms of support such as a minicom or a person to act as interpreter.

Epilepsy

This is one of the conditions most likely to affect the choice of work. A person with well-controlled epilepsy will be able to do most jobs provided there is no danger to him or herself or to others if a fit occurs. The job should always be chosen carefully for this reason. See further information in Appendix 1

Other conditions

A list of common conditions is provided in Appendix 1, with the added plea to ask the person concerned not just what the name of the condition is, but above all the effect of that condition on his or her ability to carry out the job. It is only by asking for individual detail of this sort that you will be able to provide reasonable adjustments as specified under the DDA.

MOVING TOWARDS EQUALITY

What motivates organizations to make changes?

It is to be hoped that the DDA will of itself stimulate creative changes in thinking and consequent improvements in practice with regard to employees with disabilities. But in the past the initial motivator has often been the personal experience of someone in the company. Perhaps a relative of someone senior has become disabled, or maybe a professional contact in another organization has spoken about a specific person with a disability and what has resulted from making adjustments to that person's working arrangements. The Institute of Employment Studies survey's case studies suggested that people in organizations who had themselves encountered a wide range of disabilities had a much broader image of disabled people, and were much less likely to think of stereotypical examples in discussing such issues.

Another factor which has been shown to be influential in the development of positive policies is the time available and the general level of enthusiasm of personnel staff. Maybe this explains the positive correlation between increased company size (where time allocation may be more flexible) and provision for people with disabilities. It certainly seems important to have one named individual responsible for managing the issue of disability and its place in equal opportunities in the organization (see also Chapter 5, on policies and codes). The recession of the early 1990s, and the consequent down-turn in recruitment, also ironically enabled HR managers to give some extra time to developing policies and practices on disability.

A potential problem here is the locus of ownership of equal opportunity management. Personnel professionals have an essential role to play in initiating and managing such systems, yet as Roffey Park Management Institute have found (see *People Management*, 30 November 1995) there are very few companies where HR people have worked strategically alongside line managers to bring about the necessary changes in general people management practices. There is a parallel in total quality management: unless every manager feels it is part of his or her everyday remit, rather than part of some theoretical vision espoused by top management or a specialist in the HR department, it is unlikely that changes will be implemented as effectively as possible. Again, personal interest will often play a part in the case of disability: managers who have previously worked in a team including a disabled person, or who have other relevant life experiences, can often galvanize co-workers into making improvements to practice.

Personal experience of people with disabilities can be counter-productive if people within an organization have crossed swords with some of the more militant disabled people. It is unfortunately true to say that, as in all areas of society which have been at a disadvantage, there are some people with disabilities who have reacted to this injustice by being overly aggressive. Sometimes they have understandably had difficulties in acknowledging and accepting the fact of their disability, and when this is combined with an infringement of their human rights, it is easy to see why they may behave in ways which they feel are justified but which are not conducive to smooth employer-employee relations.

However, it is important to remember that there are many more people with disabilities who have good social skills, who are intent on making their own way in the world, having relationships, having fun, and earning money just like everyone else employed by your organization. Indeed, there is anecdotal evidence that people with disabilities tend to be more motivated and loyal to their company than non-disabled people.

The business case for employing people with disabilities

There are various arguments in favour of increasing the number of disabled people in your workforce, quite apart from the legal

Table 2.2 *Perceived advantages in employing people with disabilities*

Advantage	% of employers identifying benefits who cited specific advantage
Social responsibility/equal opportunities	50.3
More committed workforce	43.3
Wider recruitment field	20.1
Raising awareness	15.3
Promotes team spirit	7.0
Fulfil legal obligations	1.0
Financial support	0.6
Unspecified	1.9
Total (N=)	314.0

Source: Honey, Meager and Williams (1993)

imperative. It is a salutary exercise to think in terms of the advantages of widening your employee base, rather than seeing it largely from the point of view of the problems that you might encounter!

If you are in an organization which aims to employ a diverse workforce as a matter of course, and has well established disability policies, you may have a clearer idea both of your personal opinion and of the view taken by your organization. The Institute for Employment Studies survey listed a number of reasons, shown in Table 2.2, in favour of employing disabled people. These are all significant factors which may serve to enhance the performance and reputation of your organization, although it is likely that the legal imperative has now crept higher up the list!

Further historical evidence to consider comes from the Du Pont survey (1973–77), which found that workers with disabilities were more safety conscious; that 91 per cent rated average or better on job performance; 79 per cent rated better on attendance, and 93 per cent rated better or average on turnover. These ratings were not affected by the severity of the disability.

Corporate social responsibility

This is an area which is being increasingly seen as central to an organization's well-being. Social responsibility encompasses a wide range of aspects, including responsibilities towards customers, shareholders,

33

the environment and the wider community, as well as towards employees themselves. All these sectors may include people with disabilities, in addition to those who support equal treatment for disabled people without necessarily being disabled themselves. The responsiveness of your company to its customer profile in particular is almost certainly a core indicator of its success in the marketplace.

Disabled customers – and others

There are two main reasons for aiming to reflect the make-up of your customer base in the composition of your workforce. First, your company will open up to a wider range of potential employees, with differing life experiences and different skills, who may add insight to your business operations. Second, you will gain points in terms of your company image. If the public perception is that your organization is fair, supportive and welcoming towards people with disabilities, whether or not they are employees, then that goodwill will show itself in customer loyalty and increased profits.

Some organizations have had booklets printed entitled *Welcoming Disabled Customers*. These little guides, obtainable from the Employers' Forum on Disability, include some simple tips on how best to serve customers who have various disabilities. They offer a practical approach to underline the core message of listening to your customers and asking them how you may best meet their needs. They also help your organization towards fulfilling its duties under the goods, facilities and services sections of the DDA (see page 149).

Building on diversity

Diversity (valuing everyone for their individuality) is a concept that in some organizations has supplanted the idea of equal opportunities. At first glance the differences between the two approaches may appear quite subtle, but from a manager's point of view the practical implications are significant.

The idea of equal opportunities arose from the experience of various groups (eg women, black people), of being less favourably treated. Equal opportunities policies have therefore traditionally been born of a determination not to discriminate against particular groups; this has often involved positive action directed at some specific sets of people. Targets are a particular example of this, and many people were glad when it was proposed that the quota on employing disabled people (Disabled Persons (Employment) Act, 1944) should be superseded by the provisions of the DDA.

Valuing diversity within your workforce means getting the most from all your employees by recognizing their individual needs and unique gifts and talents. It is rooted in a solid understanding of business objectives, based on a strong mission and fair culture. For the management of diversity to be successful, the culture must empower all individuals to reach their potential, regardless of the group to which they might belong. Kandola and Fullerton (1994) discuss the concept of diversity at length, and summarize the key differences (see Table 2.3).

Following a literature review, Kandola and Fullerton undertook a survey of diversity initiatives in companies throughout the UK. Out of 2000 organizations, 285 replied to their questionnaire, and the results make interesting reading. Flexibility proved to be a key ingredient in the implementation of successful diversity initiatives, and the business case for managing diversity was accepted, but typically not monitored or evaluated.

There were 17 items employers listed as the most compelling reasons for taking action (see Table 2.4). Note that nearly 40 per cent of respondents believed that diversity initiatives made *good business sense*.

Table 2.3 *How managing diversity is different*

Managing diversity	Equal opportunities
● ensures all employees maximize their potential and their contribution to the organization	● concentrates on issues of discrimination
● embraces a broad range of people; no-one is excluded	● perceived as an issue for women, ethnic minorities and people with disabilities
● concentrates on issues of movement within an organization, the culture of the organization and meeting business objectives	● less of an emphasis on culture change and the meeting of business objectives
● is the concern of all employees, especially managers	● seen as an issue to do with personnel and HR practitioners
● does not rely on positive action/ affirmative action	● relies on positive action

Source: Kandola and Fullerton (1994)

35

Table 2.4 *Reasons for taking action*

	%
1 Good business sense	40
2 Legislation	34
3 Senior management commitment	27
4 Good practice	11
5 Fair and caring treatment of staff/corporate values/culture	8
6 Responding to/reflecting community and consumer needs	8
7 Organizational image	7
8 Developing potential of individuals	6
9 Pressure from the centre/other parts of the organization	6
10 Pressure from members	5
11 Recruitment and retention	5
12 Morally right	4
13 Responding to needs of workforce	4
14 Personnel action	4
15 Equal opportunities department action	4
16 Better service to customer	3
17 Staff morale/relationships	2

Source: Kandola and Fullerton (1994)

Concepts and action

Diversity is an attractive concept. Table 2.4 makes it clear that companies acknowledge there is a clear business benefit to be gained from steering away from homogenous groups. It also makes intuitive sense to value individuals for themselves, rather than on the basis of their belonging to a particular group. Stereotyping is also reduced, as we strip away our tendency to categorize people. But in the context of this book – in other words, in terms of practical suggestions on implementing good practice following the DDA – it is necessary to focus on specific action for this particular group of people, ie those who have a disability under the definition in the Act. Yet if what is being recommended here is based on fairness and equal treatment, then it will be of benefit to all individuals. For example, ramps which are installed for wheelchair users are welcomed by workers pushing heavy trolleys and customers with pushchairs too! Just because people have individual differences, it does not mean that they cannot share the same organizational goals. Where there is a genuine culture of diversity, difference will be seen not as a weakness, but as a strength.

As Cox (1992) writes:

> A primary reason that we have failed to capitalize on the richness of diversity in our workforce is that learning is often one-way. The new recruit learns how to fit into the organization, but what is the organization willing to learn from the new recruit?

AN EXAMPLE OF EQUAL OPPORTUNITIES INITIATIVES

In the early days of the disability debate, Midland Bank (now HSBC Bank) produced a booklet outlining some of the many initiatives that it has developed in the areas of disability, gender and race. It includes a Foreword by the bank's Equal Opportunities Director, thus highlighting the importance accorded to the subject by the bank. The section on disability follows on from the policy statement; permission was granted by Midland Bank to reproduce it here.

Disability
Midland values the individual contribution of people irrespective of any disability. Additionally, if an existing employee becomes disabled, every effort will be made to retain them within the workforce, wherever reasonable and practical.

Community
Midland is seeking to improve its services to disabled customers and has taken a number of initiatives to support this; for example,

- Customer Focus Training for employees in branches, supported by a booklet entitled 'Welcoming Disabled Customers'.
- Braille, clear print and audio cassette versions of a range of brochures on Midland's services.
- A pilot programme of premises refurbishment to provide improved facilities for disabled people.
- Induction loops to aid communication with hearing aid wearers have been installed in all branches. A leaflet describing these and other facilities is available from branches in Braille, large print and audio cassette.

Employees

Disability Equality Action Group
An advisory group of disabled employees meets regularly to discuss disability related issues and provide direct feedback on disability issues relating to employment and customer service.

Disability Equality Training
An on-going programme of training, delivered by disabled professional trainers, is available for all levels of management. Over 400 managers and staff have already received disability equality training and courses will continue.

Disabled Employees Network
A London-based network has been established providing a forum for disabled colleagues to exchange ideas and peer group support.

Disability Symbol
Midland uses the disability symbol on all recruitment literature. This means that the Bank has undertaken to meet certain criteria laid down by the Employment Department (now the DfEE) regarding the employment of disabled people.

Good Practice
The equal opportunities unit provides information and advice on good practice in the area of disability. This includes help on disability 'etiquette', codes of practice, and videos. Evaluation of our graduate assessment centres has been undertaken to ensure selection methods are fair to disabled graduates.

Pensions
Midland's pensions are available to disabled employees on the same terms as non-disabled colleagues.

Rehabilitation Policy
Midland has a rehabilitation policy which provides an opportunity for employees who become disabled to return or continue to work. The process involves professional employment assessment and retraining wherever possible.

Work Experience
Midland encourages all areas of the Bank to provide work experience to disabled people of working age. Work experience helps to break down stereotypical assumptions about disabled people and their abilities and provides an opportunity for disabled people to enhance their job skills.

Communication with Visually Impaired People
Midland provides a range of material – eg Braille, large print and audio tape for employees. Job Application forms are also available in Braille and large print.

Communication with Deaf and Hearing Impaired People
Midland is a supporter of the Royal National Institute for Deaf People's campaign 'Louder than Words' and is committed to improving communication with deaf people.

- Midland supports the 'sympathetic hearing scheme' and displays the listening ear symbol in branches.
- A portable induction loop is available to help employees with hearing aids when attending training courses or conferences.
- A number of deaf staff have been provided with Minicom text telephones and are registered with Typetalk.

Access for Wheelchair Users
The HSBC training college at Bricket Wood, and newly built establishments, such as our processing centres, are wheelchair accessible.

Special Equipment/Adaptations
Most disabled people do not need special equipment or adaptations, but sometimes provision of these can help an employee to operate more effectively at work. Midland makes use of the Employment Department schemes when employees' needs are identified.

Employers' Networks
Midland is a Board member of the Employers' Forum on Disability, the only national employers' organisation concerned exclusively with the training and employment of people with disabilities.

Employers' Agenda on Disability – Ten Points for Action
Launched by the Prime Minister in 1992, Midland was one of 21 leading UK companies to adopt an 'Employers' Agenda', drawn up by the Employers' Forum on Disability to provide a blueprint of best practice. Midland has agreed to focus on monitoring the employment of disabled people; equality training and rehabilitation and retraining initiatives.

Sponsorship
Midland continues to sponsor employment related activities in the area of disability. Examples of these have been:

- The Employers' Forum on Disability publication *Monitoring Disability in the Workplace.*
- Working with the Coverdale Organisation on a bursary programme, to provide management training opportunities for disabled people.

- Midland has provided core funding and support to the Fast Track programme, a Scope (formerly Spastics Society) initiative, to provide management training to disabled high fliers.
- Support for *New Perspectives* (Brading, J, 1996), a publication of Skill: National Bureau for Students with Disabilities.

The booklet then goes on to cover other equal opportunity areas such as family friendly policies, and initiatives with regard to race and gender. The final paragraph of the booklet gives the addresses and telephone numbers of staff members who may be contacted for more information.

CHECKLIST: CHAPTER 2

1. Do you have a named person with overall responsibility for initiating equal opportunities strategies with regard to disability? Does every manager own the implementation?

2. Have you considered the extent to which your customer base includes people with disabilities? How do you reflect that in your employee profile?

3. Do you welcome disabled customers? How could you help your team work more proactively on this issue?

4. What do you think are/would be the advantages to your organization of employing more people with disabilities?

5. Which concept is most fitting to your current organizational approach: equal opportunities or diversity? Is that how you want it to be?

3

Communication and disability

SETTING THE SCENE

A determination to create the best possible atmosphere in which all workers are able to give of their best implies some active management of the culture of your team.

Increasingly nowadays the organization may be seen as an open system, with loose boundaries and, one hopes, a growing element of cross-functional integration. Empowering people with disabilities to play their part to maximum effect involves looking first of all at what might get in the way of this: in other words, what are the potential barriers?

The typical organization has evolved organically: a result of the people within it influencing its development. For most people, potential barriers to change and growth are either accepted or worked around, depending on the importance attached to them by the individual. The system is there and accessible to those who wish to influence it.

But people with disabilities may not even get that far. Even if obvious physical barriers, such as a desk being too high, are addressed, you cannot be confident that a disabled person will feel that he or she has the same amount of power or influence as the next person. This is often because the effects of other people's attitudes are disabling in themselves: in other words, social or attitudinal barriers may seem just as impenetrable and disempowering to a person with disabilities as the lack of an adapted lift is for wheelchair users.

Understanding where these barriers originated is important. We need to look at how disability has historically been perceived, and how disabled people and their supporters are encouraging us to see it today.

THREE APPROACHES TO DISABILITY

The medical model is the approach people take when they want to talk about diagnosis, cure and what is normal and abnormal. In fact, the very idea of a cure is irrelevant or even offensive to some people with disabilities. An employee with a disability, of whatever sort, is probably not going to warm to this approach, since it implies greater power on the part of the cure-giver and those who align themselves with normality, and a complete disregard of any equal rights argument.

The tragedy model is linked to the medical model, but takes it one step further: beyond facts and diagnosis into emotive language. Indeed, the use of particular words is crucial here. If you have ever heard anyone in your organization say something like, 'Poor Alice, she's so brave, working those long hours when we all know she's a cancer victim', you will now be aware that they were approaching Alice's disability from this perspective. At first sight, it seems sympathetic, but what is really happening is that the speaker is taking an essentially disempowering stance towards the person with the disability. Alice may not want to be seen in this way: it is rather patronizing. It also separates her from her co-workers in a negative way, and will tend not to enhance her ability to make adult choices in the best interests of herself and her team. People who feel that they are being viewed as victims can react in two ways: they can acquiesce and surrender their equal status, or they can become defensive and even aggressive in their attempt to reassert their right to the same treatment as anyone else. Neither reaction is to be encouraged in the workplace.

The social model is the view of disability which is supported by many disabled people themselves (although there is increasing evidence of a backlash against this now). This model is underpinned by the belief that we all have a right to equal treatment and opportunities, no matter what our individual differences may be. It follows from this that all barriers must be removed. This includes blocks resulting from people's attitudes as well as those which prevent full access to information, services and other aspects of everyday living, which the DDA seeks to address.

The language associated with the three approaches is shown in Figure 3.1.

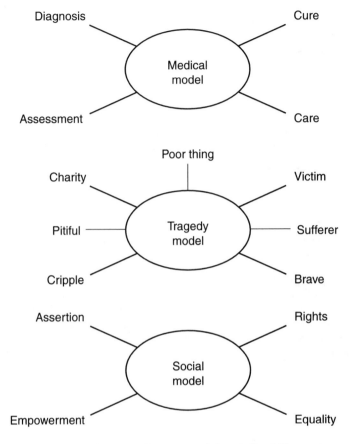

Figure 3.1 *Different models of disability*

TAKING DOWN THE BARRIERS: DISABILITY AWARENESS TRAINING

One of the best ways of making everyone aware of the issues involved in equality of opportunity for people with disabilities is to provide one-day workshops on disability awareness. These should ideally be made available to everyone, but ought really to start with senior management, to reflect the importance given to the subject.

Most people can think of times when they have been treated unfairly. The sense of impotence and frustration that accompanies such an experience can be very powerful. Sometimes these feelings can be used creatively as a trigger for action. Most good workshops on disability awareness will key into these personal experiences, enabling participants to learn more directly and lastingly, and helping them in the process of transferring their individual knowledge into action beneficial to the organization.

Organizing some training

In deciding how to set about establishing a programme of disability awareness training, there are various things to consider. These include:

- Who should be trained?
- How much money can you afford to spend?
- How would this initiative fit the organization-wide approach?
- What support do you have?

There is also the question of who will carry out the training.

How to do it

You can buy in outside training from an equal opportunities or diversity consultant, who may or may not customize their workshop to your needs. Another option is to do the training in-house, following a targeted training needs analysis and identification of aims

Table 3.1 *External or in-house training?*

External	In-house
May be expensive	Sunk cost
May not be in tune with company needs and values	Culturally congruent
Unknown quantity	The devil you know
Novelty may be inspiring	May be seen as 'just another course'
May raise visible importance of issue	Familiarity may encourage cosiness
May be seen as tokenism	Closer links with senior management may support follow-through
Valuable specialist expertise	Knowledge of specific company issues

and objectives. Some of the things to consider in deciding which approach to use are shown in Table 3.1.

You can find a list of equal opportunity/diversity trainers in the *Diversity Directory,* published by Diversity UK (see Appendix 4).

You might find the NAOMIE model (see Figure 3.2) helpful in facilitating your thinking about providing a training course on disability awareness.

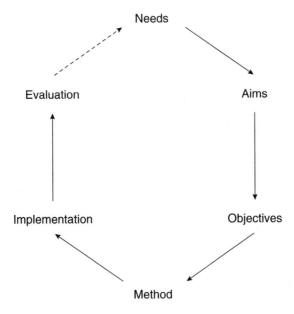

Figure 3.2 *Designing a training course*
(With acknowledgements to Pete Francis)

Cascading good practice in training

The foundation of all good training is a thorough needs analysis. It may be that the DDA has given you a prompt in this direction; that constitutes an externally imposed need. However, pressures from within your organization to make the best possible use of present and future employees will also contribute towards your assessment of your training needs.

Involving existing disabled employees in the planning is a good idea, since through consulting them you may find out about barriers which are organization-specific. You will also avoid the possible charge of making assumptions about what disabled people need. Since one in ten of the population has a disability, the chances are that you will be talking to people with disabilities, even if you are not aware of the fact!

Having assessed the need for training and who is to benefit, a set of clear aims and learning objectives will help you in deciding the method to use. When it comes to implementing your plan – in other words, actually delivering the training – don't forget to let your good practice in offering the workshops extend to how you run your group. Provide a model for equal opportunities by bearing the following hints in mind:

- find out beforehand from participants whether they have any particular needs, eg an induction loop, large print handouts, physical access requirements;
- on the day, check whether anyone needs any additional arrangements made, eg changing position so that the flipchart is more visible;
- if you yourself have a disability, use it in a positive way, eg if you are hard of hearing, ask the group not to talk all at once;
- be sure to bear in mind disability etiquette and preferred language (see below) as you prepare and deliver your course;
- include space on the evaluation sheets for suggested improvements to people's ability to access all aspects of the training experience.

Evaluating the success of the training and the validity of the workshop can be put to good use as part of your organization's approach to managing diversity in the workplace. Even if at first glance some of these suggestions seem a little superfluous for you, perhaps because no one has said that they have a disability, it is still important to use opportunities such as training to raise the general level of awareness of disability and equal opportunity within the company. Monitoring initiatives such as this can give you valuable information on which to build a company-wide approach to providing reasonable adjustments, thereby enhancing your ability to get the most from your workers.

DEALING WITH RESISTANCE:
360° COMMITMENT

Sometimes there is resistance to promoting good practice on disability. You might find people saying they haven't got the time to think about that kind of thing: they don't have any problems in that area anyway.

Maybe people with disabilities on your staff are themselves a little cynical, or worried about their disability becoming too prominent an issue.

Encourage resisters to talk openly about their reluctance. You may wish to bear in mind here what Gerard Egan has referred to as 'the shadow side' (*Management Today*, September 1993), which he defines as:

> all those things that substantially and consistently affect the productivity and quality of the working life of the business, for better or for worse, but which are not found on organisation charts, in company manuals, or in the discussions that take place in formal meetings.

This side of an organization or team, often referred to as the 'politics' or 'culture', can have enormous economic consequences for a company if not managed constructively. Egan explains:

> Companies formulate strategies, and then consistently fail to provide the kind of strategic management system needed to drive them into the guts of the organisation. The result? Strategy floats like cream on the top of a liqueur. It drives little. There is a double cost here: the wasted cost of formulating the strategy, and the lost-opportunity cost of an unimplemented or poorly implemented strategy.

It is the same with equal opportunities or diversity management. In order to be able to provide reasonable adjustments, as required by the DDA, it is essential to have the backing of not only the people at the top of the company but also your peers and the people who work for you. If they believe that they do not really have a part to play, or that no benefits are going to accrue to them or their colleagues, you will find it almost impossible to put in place an effective equal opportunity programme. The values embedded in diversity management need to be not only espoused, but also enacted.

The importance of people's personal experiences of being treated unfairly is referred to in the section on training. If in the process of looking at how people with disabilities might be treated in your organization or team, you are able to harness people's individual knowledge and imagination at the policy-making stage, you will find that goodwill and commitment are increased and resistance lessened. Similarly, if you are clear about the business arguments for employing and developing people with disabilities (see Chapter 2), you will have a stronger case for carrying out your duties under the legislation.

WHAT PRICE POLITICAL CORRECTNESS?

We seem to live in a post-pc era! More and more writers and comedians, including disabled people, have swung away from political correctness in their portrayal of people with disabilities, not to mention women and people from ethnic minorities. Suddenly it seems more acceptable, or even desirable, to poke fun at others – or so the media would suggest.

In a way, this is not all to the detriment of people with disabilities. There has been a lot of tension and rigidity associated with pc ways of talking and behaving, which has made political correctness a focus of derision. A little more humour can pave the way to fresh ideas and appraisal, without the clogging nature of political correctness jargon.

However, there are certain ways of speaking and behaving which are to be encouraged in all areas of life, as they accord people the respect they deserve as fellow human beings. A list such as the one shown in Table 3.2 may also give you some confidence if you are not used to being with people with disabilities.

PREFERRED LANGUAGE

It is easy to fall into the trap of using words which offend people with disabilities, without realizing that you are doing so. For this

Table 3.2 *Recommended language*

DO use	DON'T use
disability	handicap
people with disabilities	the disabled
disabled people	victims of . . .
wheelchair user	wheelchair bound
people with learning difficulties	mentally handicapped
people with visual impairments	visually handicapped
blind people	
partially sighted people	
deaf or hard of hearing people	deaf and dumb; deaf mute
people with mental health problems	the psychiatrically disturbed
mental health service users	the mentally ill
toilets for people with disabilities	disabled toilets
hearing aids	deaf aids
people who have diabetes, etc	people suffering from diabetes, etc

reason we include a list (see Table 3.2) of words and phrases which are recommended as being acceptable to disabled people.

Finally, do not worry about using sentences such as, 'Please come and see us again soon' if you are talking to a blind person. It is unlikely that they would take offence, as this is such a well-used phrase and does not carry with it any of the connotations associated with the terms in the right-hand column of Table 3.2, which are mainly to do with seeing the person with a disability in a less favourable light than yourself.

SOME TIPS ON MEETING SOMEONE WITH A DISABILITY

- Don't make assumptions about the person's needs. Offer help if it seems appropriate, but be guided by him or her.
- Don't get stuck on medical diagnoses or labels. These may well be irrelevant to the task in hand.
- Be aware of personal space. If talking to a wheelchair user, for example, don't lean on the wheelchair.
- Don't be hesitant about shaking hands or making eye contact. Reduce unease by smiling.
- Ask the person you are speaking to about communication. Adapt your practice to suit what is easiest for him or her.
- If you are with a deaf person and an interpreter is present, remember to speak and look at the person rather than the interpreter, difficult though this may seem. You will notice that the deaf person will not be able to maintain eye contact with you, but will have to watch the interpreter: don't allow yourself to be disconcerted by this. Speak clearly with the light falling on your face, so that you are clearly visible.
- With a blind person, introduce yourself and anyone else clearly, explaining where in the room everyone is. Say, 'Shall we shake hands?' if that seems appropriate. Offer him or her your arm for guidance and when you reach a chair, place the person's hand on the back of it.
- Be encouraging but not patronizing. Never finish sentences for people. Give them time and respect.
- If in doubt about anything, ask the person concerned.

THE COMPETENT MANAGER OF DISABLED PEOPLE

Dealing with the issues of disability awareness-raising and resistance management, and providing a role model for speaking and behaving in a way that mirrors your valuing of individual differences, are all aspects of your job as a manager. Some authors have concluded that what they refer to as managerial 'diversity competence' is based on qualities such as the following, from McEnroe (1993):

- the capacity to accept the relativity of one's own knowledge and perceptions;
- the capacity to be non-judgmental;
- a tolerance for ambiguity;
- the capacity to appreciate and communicate respect for other people's ways, backgrounds, values and beliefs;
- the capacity to demonstrate empathy;
- the capacity to be flexible;
- a willingness to acquire new patterns of behaviour and belief;
- the humility to acknowledge what one does not know.

All these qualities and skills are the same as those needed for effective management in *any* context, irrespective of whether diversity is the conscious backdrop. Communication, self-awareness and valuing other people are essential tools in any manager's kitbag. They need to underpin any organizational attempt to create and manage a diverse workforce.

CHECKLIST: CHAPTER 3

1. Think of typical tasks or scenarios which might occur in the work-life of your team. List the barriers that a person with a particular disability might come up against, on three levels:

   - physical barriers (eg doorways);
   - individual attitudes;
   - cultural aspects ('the way we do things round here').

2. Have you thought through possible ways of ensuring that your people have access to disability awareness training? What about putting on some 'Opportunity from diversity' workshops?

3. Are you confident that you have the expertise in-house to provide such training? If not, talk to people experienced in this area (see the *Diversity Directory*, published by Diversity UK).

4. Have you thought through what to do about resistance? Involving everyone is helpful – if people *own* the initiatives, they are more likely to be positive.

4

Employing disabled people

BEING FAIR: RECRUITMENT AND SELECTION

Those employers who fail to provide opportunities for people with disabilities do so partly because of their own prejudices and misunderstandings but also because of their traditional recruitment practices. Unless they can be persuaded to alter their views and recruitment procedures, it is argued, employers will continue to be unable to understand the value of employees with disabilities and will not consider them for employment (Duckworth, 1993).

As a general rule, the more you communicate your intentions and your philosophy, and embed them in the way work is carried out on a daily basis, the easier other people will find it to carry out your policy. Fair selection should be based upon only one thing: the ability (or potential ability) of the person to do the job. Making this simple fact known can take you a long way along the road towards ensuring equality of opportunity.

Reasonable adjustments

It is worth mentioning here that recruitment, as well as every other aspect of employment, is subject to the requirements of the DDA that employers have a positive duty to make reasonable adjustments to working arrangements or to the workplace to counter any substantial disadvantages that a disabled applicant or employee might have. This is dealt with more fully in Chapter 7, and examples are given of what might be done and what is likely to constitute reasonableness. We would also recommend that you follow the suggestions in the *Code of Practice on Employment*, available from the Stationery Office (see Chapter 5).

Employers Must Plan Ahead

Williams v *Channel 5 Engineering Services Ltd*

Christian Williams, who is profoundly deaf, applied for a job as a Channel 5 re-tuner. At the beginning of January 1997, he began a three-day training course. He passed the test on the first two days. However, the third day involved a video with no subtitles. He was refused one-to-one training with the trainer and left without sitting the final day's test. On 15 January, he was provided with one-to-one training and he passed the course. However, the training delay led to a delay in obtaining his ID card. When it was issued, the necessary special aid had not been obtained. Further delay ensued, by which time the re-tuning programme was running down, and the need for re-tuners was ceasing. As a result, Mr Williams was never employed. He claimed unlawful discrimination.

A London South industrial tribunal (Chair: J Gilbert) upheld the claim. It found that the failure to make adjustments to the training course at the beginning of January was a basic act of discrimination on the grounds of disability which directly led to a delay in obtaining his ID card, by which time the vacant re-tuner slots had been filled. The tribunal rejected the employer's argument that no duty to make an adjustment arose until the applicant had passed his training.

The whole tenor of the Act read with the Code of Practice is that employers should avoid discrimination and plan ahead by considering the needs of future disabled employees. Steps to obtain necessary equipment for training and deployment should have have been initiated when Channel 5 embarked on the re-tuning programme including provision in the application form used by the recruitment agencies to state whether an applicant was in any way disabled and if so, in what respect.

24 October 1997; case no. 2302136/97.

Job descriptions

However you decide to arrive at a job description – whether it's by asking the present incumbent to keep a record of tasks, or whether you are basing it on a critical incident approach – the essential point is that only the relevant job criteria should be included. You will need to take care that any unnecessary requirements or restrictions are excluded. For example, if it is necessary for someone to be independently mobile, then this is what should be stated, rather than that driving is an essential part of the job. Try to step outside the box and be creative: how inflexible are the working hours *really*? Is the post suitable for job-sharing? Consider ways in which you could adapt the job and its conditions so that it may become suitable for a wider range of applicants than, for example, those who want to work from nine to five.

The more tightly you are able to construct the job description, the better your position, both in terms of ensuring you hire the right person for the job, and as regards the possibility of defending your actions in the case of a complaint (see specimen questionnaire on pages 142–46).

Job Rejection Justified

Fozard v Greater Manchester Police Authority

Ms Fozard has congenital myotonic dystrophy. This caused reduced manual dexterity and learning difficulties as a child. She is registered disabled and deemed to have a disability for the purposes of the DDA. In early 1997 she applied for a temporary post of word-processor operator with the respondent police authority. She filled in the application form stating that she had a registered disability and answered the question about special needs in the negative. One of the essential criteria for the job was accuracy in written work. However, her application form contained a number of errors and she was rejected. A Manchester industrial tribunal (Chair: A F W Wooley) dismissed her disability discrimination claim. It accepted that the reason for rejection related to the applicant's disability, but held that the treatment was justified. In its view, the reason why the respondent was looking for accuracy in written work was 'that it was part of the job to create type-written records and minutes of meetings and other documents' and filling in the application form was a fair test of accuracy. This reason, said the tribunal, 'was material to the circumstances and substantial'.

The tribunal rejected the submission that the employer should have taken steps to find out whether the applicant's lack of accuracy was related to the disability in order to make any adjustments necessary such as providing a spell-check facility. In its view:

> [the employer's] question about the applicant's needs on the form was the proper and reasonably practicable means whereby they attempted to ascertain whether they should make some adjustment in accordance with s.6. As the applicant did not suggest that she would be at a substantial disadvantage without a spell-check facility, we accept the respondents did not know that she was likely to be affected in the way mentioned in s.6(1) of the Act.

12 June 1997; case no. 24011143/97.

Person specifications

Being able to describe the sort of person you want to undertake the job involves identifying the necessary competencies and performance criteria. It is at this stage particularly that you have the power to create equal opportunities for potential applicants.

The usual things people think about when creating a person specification are listed here, with some suggestions on further matters to take into account to ensure you are able to attract a diverse range of people. Both essential and desirable criteria need to be itemized, either as a competency-based list, or under the following headings:

- education standard;
- qualifications;
- experience;
- personal qualities or skills.

Every item in the person specification must be:

- relevant to the effective performance of the job as set out in the job description;
- measurable by agreed methods;
- legal and in line with the organization's employment policies and practices.

The sticking points in the above lists concern unexamined expectations and our natural tendency to hire in our own image (hence the prevalence of homogenous groups). People with disabilities may, for example, have a non-traditional educational background, so stop and think: how relevant and essential to the job in question are those taken-for-granted qualifications? Could it be held to be discriminatory if you include as part of your person specification requirements that are over-inflationary, and not tightly linked to the job description? In the same way that age limits will themselves restrict your choice of applicants, so the more subtle decisions about inclusion and exclusion of irrelevant criteria will create a false balance in your short list of candidates.

No Adjustment Reasonably Practicable

Matty v Tesco Stores Ltd

Mr Matty, a diabetic, applied for a job as a fitter at Tesco's distribution centre in Hinkley. The job involved fitters working alone on an irregular shift rota, the climbing of ladders up to 40 feet and having to spend several

---

hours a week working in an environment of –25°C. In the light of advice from the company's occupational health adviser that a diabetic employed as a fitter would be at risk and following consideration of reasonable adjustments, the company, whilst accepting that he was the best candidate, rejected Mr Matty's application. He unsuccessfully claimed unlawful discrimination. A Leicester industrial tribunal found that the failure to make an adjustment was justified.

> As far as the premises are concerned, no adjustment was reasonably practicable. The racking could not be lowered to a height at which it would be safe to allow the applicant to work and the freezer could not be run at a higher temperature. Equipment, such as protective clothing, was supplied to all staff who were required to work in the freezer. It was the best, but, although it had the highest tog rating available, staff still felt the cold. They had to be given frequent warm-up periods. The nature of the fitter's job was that, in an emergency, he might have to spend long periods carrying out work in and on the freezer. As a diabetic, the risk of his sustaining injury from such work was increased and the risk could not be reduced by supplying or modifying equipment. There was no way in which the nature of the job could be changed. For reasons of cost, it was not possible to have two fitters on duty all the time, thereby allowing the applicant to work in ambient temperature and on the ground. Altering his hours would not help.

30 October 1997; case no. 1901114/97

Here is an example of how to deal with the difficult question of assessing a person's ability to do the job in question, without asking discriminatory or unnecessary questions. It comes from an American journal, and is from an article examining the impact of the Americans with Disabilities Act on selection procedures.

> Consider the example of a position which requires an employee to be able to lift fifty pound boxes to waist-level height. Assume that the job analysis has demonstrated that the ability to do so is moderately important for employment. An interviewer cannot (under American law) ask applicants if they have back or blood pressure problems that might interfere with their lifting ability. Neither can an interviewer simply assume that a disabled applicant (for example, an applicant in a wheelchair) lacks the ability. However the interviewer can ask the applicant whether he or she can perform the function (lifting) at the level required on the job (low, moderate or high). A standardised screening and selection process might even include work-sample exercises that would directly test the applicant's ability, so long as the job analysis had demonstrated that the ability was essential to the position (and so long as the exercise was applied to all applicants for the job). (Hollwitz et al., 1995)

Using a range of selection techniques

The most commonly used techniques are listed and defined below.

- *Ability tests*. Short paper and pencil measures of specific cognitive abilities or attainments like numeracy, spelling, verbal reasoning, etc.
- *Assessment centres*. These involve combinations of exercises, tests and interviews. They usually last one to three days, and ratings are made by trained observers. The objective is to choose the most long-term promotable candidates from a range of eligible candidates.
- *Astrology*. Knowledge of someone's birth sign. (Yes, some companies do use it!)
- *Biodata*. Biographical data about someone's age, position in family, hobbies, habits, etc.
- *Graphology*. Assessment based on analysis of someone's handwriting.
- *Personality inventories*. Structured tests based on true/false answers or similar.
- *References*. Letters of recommendation from previous employers, supervisors or teachers.
- *Structured interviews*. Face-to-face interviews in which questions are prepared and follow a very clear sequence.
- *Typical interviews*. Face-to-face interviews without many prepared questions and in which the strategy for questioning is decided from moment to moment.
- *Work sample tests*. Typing, manual dexterity, report writing or some other example of the mastery of current work.

(Source: Oxford Psychologists Press.)

All these may be subject to the reasonable adjustment provisions in the Act.

Recruitment advertising

If, in the interests of diversity, you want to cast your net as widely as possible, there are various points to consider. First, how does your company present itself to the outside world? If you are trying to hire graduates for example, and your glossy and expensive brochures only have pictures of young, white able-bodied men or women, and equal opportunities or disability are mentioned almost as an afterthought, you will probably find that people with disabilities are not attracted to you. If, on the other hand, you make full use of the 'Positive about disabled people' symbol (see page 59 and Chapter 6), and you stress the flexibility of your organization in the broadest sense by mentioning such things as family-friendly policies and career breaks, you will find that you are able to select from a much wider range of applicants. *But only do this if you are willing to follow it through!* Recruitment literature is a marvellous opportunity to broadcast your organizational values: just make sure that your everyday practice follows your policies.

A measure of an organization's commitment to recruiting more people with disabilities can be taken by looking at where the advertising is being placed. Using the disability press, such as the newspaper *Disability Now*, from Scope, can help ensure that what you want to say reaches the widest audience. Similarly, building a relationship with your local disability employment adviser at the jobcentre (see page 109), and ensuring that all vacancies are notified to them, can be very productive. In addition, belonging to a local employer network on disability, or the national Employers' Forum on Disability, can provide you with a source of new ideas and methods of being proactive in your recruitment strategy. See Chapter 6 for more suggestions.

The language you use in the advertisements needs to be carefully chosen. We include suggestions on the use of words in Chapter 3; in the case of constructing advertisements, sensitivity to the *effect* of your language is necessary. For example, be clear about what are and are not attractive forms of words to use in describing your approach to equal opportunities. The 1996 Austin Knight survey, *Equality at Work*, found that an overwhelming majority of people want to see equal opportunity statements as part of recruitment advertisements, and that the statement seen in the most favourable light by all groups was:

> We welcome applications regardless of race, colour, disability, marital status or sex.

In a sense, the popularity of this statement is curious, since it would seem to exclude other untenable reasons for discrimination, such as religious affiliation, but that was indeed the statement favoured by 79.2 per cent of the Austin Knight sample. The statement seen as least likely to encourage all groups to apply was:

> We only discriminate on ability.

This is puzzling since this is in fact the statement that most closely matches the belief held by diversity enthusiasts!

For more information on policy statements and codes, see Chapter 5.

The symbol

Employers who use the Employment Service 'Positive about disabled people' symbol (the 'two ticks' symbol) are publicly showing their commitment to taking positive measures. More information on the symbol and its uses are given in Chapter 6, but it is worth remembering that your use or not of the symbol will have an effect on how people who are attuned to the subject of equal opportunities perceive your organization, and this could have wider ramifications than just in the disability arena.

Other ways of attracting people with disabilities

Many organizations use on-line services to advertise vacancies. This is fine, as long as you bear in mind that if some automatic preliminary selection is being carried out on your behalf, it is important to satisfy yourself that any sifting procedures are not in themselves discriminatory, for example, by sorting people *unnecessarily* according to their academic qualifications. (This holds good for your use of agencies or head-hunters too.)

A potential trap for unwary managers advertising posts (and this can apply to internally displayed notices too) is as follows.

Where a job is advertised, and a disabled person who applies is refused or deliberately not offered it and complains to an employment tribunal about disability discrimination, the Act requires the tribunal to assume (unless the employer can prove otherwise) that the reason the person did not get the job was related to his or her disability if the advertisement could reasonably be taken to indicate:

- that the success of a person's application for the job might depend to any extent on the absence of disability such as the applicant's; or

- that the employer is unwilling to make an adjustment for a disabled person.

(Source: Code of Practice on Employment, Section 5.7.)

So if you include something like 'access to our offices can be awkward for people with mobility difficulties', the onus would be on you to prove that a person, say in a wheelchair, was refused the job for a reason unconnected with their disability.

WHAT HAPPENS IN PRACTICE?

The Institute of Employment Studies survey, *Employers' Attitudes to People with Disabilities*, found the following methods of recruitment used:

Among those organizations actively seeking to recruit people with disabilities, nearly half indicated that they did this for all vacancies. Very few organizations with a pro-active recruitment strategy limited recruiting people with disabilities to a specified range of vacancies. The questionnaire also examined how such organizations went about attracting job applicants with disabilities. The two most frequently used methods were job advertisements welcoming disabled applicants, and notification of vacancies to the Employment Service [ES] disability specialists, both of which approaches were used by approximately half of these respondents. A third of respondents who actively recruited disabled people used the Employment Service disability symbol in their literature.

The case studies also confirmed that although most organizations did approach either Jobcentres or use the ES services in this context, there was a wide range of other methods being employed, such as open days, recruitment fairs, and establishing links with disability organizations. Many organizations had also revised their general recruitment practices, eg by training all recruitment staff in equal opportunity issues; revising application forms and using new employee starter forms; drawing up much tighter job descriptions and person specifications; operating guaranteed interview schemes and offering work experience and training schemes.

Application forms or CVs?

People with disabilities sometimes dread filling in application forms! This is especially true of those forms which equate disability and ill health, and which seem perversely to hinder the articulation of a person's strengths and abilities. Some people believe that the most effective way of enabling someone to give of their best on an application form, at the same time as circumventing possible stereotyping by readers of the form, is to keep the personal details (even the person's name) on a separate, detachable piece of paper. This form is needed for monitoring purposes, and can include questions about gender, age, ethnic group, disability and care for dependants. These are facts you as a recruiter will need to know, in order to evaluate the extent to which your advertising is penetrating different sections of the labour market, but at the initial stages of selection these details are irrelevant. The only aspects of a person's ability you need to judge are those directly related to the job description and person specification.

Some lawyers advise, however, that since the implementation of the DDA, it is possible that employers whose selection procedures take no account of disability at the first sift could be said to be acting unlawfully by indirectly discriminating against a disabled applicant, even though the process is aimed at treating all applicants equally. You will need to judge how best to balance the two sides of the argument in your own selection procedures.

Many organizations require all applications to be made on company forms and if this applies to you, you must make sure that these are correctly designed and worded, as above. Even if this is the case, you may still find that you are sent some CVs, maybe on a speculative basis. Many people with disabilities prefer to use CVs anyway, because they are thereby given more control over how they present their disability. There is evidence to suggest that people who are candid about their disabilities suffer more discrimination from employers than those who choose to delay disclosure until they are further along the recruitment path into an organization. This is a tricky area for both sides, particularly as trust between employer and employee is essential. The way to encourage discussion of disability is to ensure that your public image is welcoming to all applicants, having regard only for people's ability to do the job in question. Again, you need to be aware of your duty of reasonable adjustment (mentioned above) which applies to all parts of the selection process.

Practical example: recruitment

If you want people with a disability to apply to your organization and be clear to you about what their support needs are, you will need to make it obvious to them that their disability is not going to stand in their way.

A major retailer states in advertisements that they recognize that if 10 per cent of the workforce are disabled, then not all the most talented people will be in the other 90 per cent! They encourage diversity, believing that homogenous groups do not work as creatively as varied teams and that in addition, people with a disability bring a fresh perspective to work with customers. To ensure fairness in the selection process, they guarantee that their recruiters are trained in disability awareness, and that all decisions are based on merit alone. All these facts have been clearly stated in advertisements, which are always accompanied by the 'two ticks' symbol.

PSYCHOMETRIC TESTING

As the search for the perfect means of assessing people continues, more and more emphasis is being placed on methods other than the traditional interview. In selection particularly, psychometric testing is used routinely by some companies.

The advantages of using psychometrics are clear and established. Perhaps the main benefit is that, providing a thorough job analysis has been completed and you can be sure that what you are attempting to measure is a real job requirement *and* you have a test that can give you that information, then candidate results may easily be compared with relevant normative information, and certain predictions may be made. This means, in effect, that using tests as part of a standardized selection procedure can give an extremely valuable insight into people's abilities and potential to fit into your team.

But all the above is based on an assumption: that everyone may be made to fit into one of the tested norm groups for the purposes of comparison. Using psychometric tests on people with disabilities may in some cases lead to inaccurate results if no provision for the disability has been made.

Psychometric instruments such as interest inventories or personality tests do not present much difficulty. Once you have sorted out any access problems for the candidates (for example, by providing large print questionnaires) the results you end up with will be valuable in the sense of adding to your knowledge of the candidate's preferences and characteristics. Because these types of test results are not open to comparison with norm groups in the way that ability or attainment tests are, the disabled candidate will not suffer any disadvantage as a result of interpretation.

In the case of ability or attainment tests, there is a danger that unless allowance for the effects of a person's disability is made, test results will give a false picture. The problem is that test administration procedures need to be standardized for the test results to carry any validity. Comparisons with norm groups cannot be made unless all the conditions associated with test taking are consistent. However, people with certain disabilities may, by the nature of the standard administration procedures, be excluded from fair assessment. If you, as an employer, want to ensure that you provide reasonable adjustments to test taking for disabled people, then you must take some extra steps. A major test producer, SHL (1993), recommends the following.

Before inviting candidates to the session:

- Ask the candidate about the disability and how he/she copes with it
- Provide the candidate with a practice leaflet;
- Ask the candidate if he/she anticipates any problems in taking the tests and how these might be overcome;
- Consult the test producer regarding best test procedures;
- Make arrangements for an appropriate venue;
- Make sure any additional equipment or facilities required are available;
- Ensure that the candidate can get to the venue.

(Copyright material of SHL (UK) Ltd and reproduced with their kind permission.)

Because people with disabilities do not form a homogenous group, it is impossible to create a template for your approach to this subject. But perhaps you can make it easier for yourself if you build a matrix (as in Table 4.1) which you can fill in for each person. This is one way of focusing your thinking. Obviously this matrix may be added to and amended to suit each individual.

To sum up, psychometric testing can be a great bonus in fair selection and assessment because it can bypass biases arising from stereotyping. People with disabilities may have an equal chance of showing their capabilities, even if they have a non-traditional educational background. But in order to ensure that your tests are equally valuable for individual disabled candidates, some simple steps such as those outlined above may help you in your role as selector or assessor and will help you ensure you work to the 'reasonable adjustments' duty.

Practical example: testing

Many people with dyslexia do not even discover that this is the case until they come up against a situation such as the following.

Sally's dyslexia came to light when it became clear that, although she had great numerical ability, her verbal reasoning test scores were very poor. She was a student at the time and worried that potential employers might also be put off by her bad A-level results (even though she eventually got a first in her degree). In her pre-finals search for a job, she was advised by her university careers advisory service to contact the companies before sitting any tests, and arrange for extra time. Sally was ambivalent about this, since she felt that to a certain extent she would be relying on the organizations' goodwill. She therefore made a decision not to ask for extra time when faced with psychometric testing, believing that to do so would make more of an issue of her dyslexia. After making many applications and sitting through some unsuccessful test sessions, she finally found herself being interviewed by someone whose child was dyslexic and who therefore had an interest in the subject. She was offered the job and is now successfully employed as a systems analyst.

Table 4.1 *Example of testing arrangements matrix*

		Type of disability			
		Visual	**Hearing**	**Motor**	**Other – specified**
	Communication		Is a signer required?		
General issues	Mobility			Are there ramps/lifts/ difficult stairs, etc?	
	Facilities			Wheelchair facilities?	
	Pre-testing	Should a practice run be organized?			
Testing	Instructions	Braille?			
	The test	Braille?			Extra time?
	Other selection methods	Outward bound course – is extra assistance required?			

Under the DDA, companies using psychometric testing as part of their selection process will be obliged to make reasonable adjustments to accommodate people like Sally. Doing so, and making it clear in their recruitment literature and at interviews that they do so, will ensure that they avail themselves of all the possible talent that exists among job-seekers.

The Disability Rights Task Force, set up to recommend terms of reference for the Disability Rights Commission, had three suggestions to make:

5.32 Disability or disability-related enquiries before a job is offered should be permitted only in limited circumstances:

- when inviting someone for interview or to take a selection test, employers could ask if someone had a disability that may require reasonable adjustments to the selection process; and
- when interviewing, employers would be allowed to ask job-related questions, including if someone had a disability which might mean a reasonable adjustment would be required.

Further consideration should be given to other circumstances where such enquiries should be permitted, for instance, for monitoring purposes, with rules on confidentiality of information obtained, and in the particular case of the guaranteed interview scheme.

5.33 Except in the circumstances in recommendation 5.32, disability or disability-related enquiries should only take place, where justified, when a job offer, conditional on passing a medical or other test, has been made.

ASSESSMENT AND DEVELOPMENT CENTRES (AC/DC)

The core advice here is the same as in many of the sections in this book: ask the individual what his or her needs are, and interpret the results of the assessment in the context of what the person can do, as demonstrated elsewhere.

Having said that, you will find it useful to gather information from your own experience of assessing people with disabilities and from contacting specialist organizations who might be able to advise you. Some of these are listed at the back of this book. If you are using an external organization to run your assessment centre, you may find that it already has a bank of information and experience on which to draw.

An important issue is to ensure that the people running the assessment centre are properly trained with regard to disability (see Chapter 3) and that as many potential difficulties as possible are pre-empted. A typical assessment or development centre is characterized by a standardized evaluation of behaviour based on multiple inputs. As with psychometric testing, there is evidence that a carefully designed AC or DC provides strong objective data on which to base selection or development decisions. In their booklet, *Guidelines for best practice in the use of assessment and development centres*, SHL (1993) include a section on equal opportunities in general, which is helpful when considering specific issues to do with people with disabilities:

> The following points should be considered to ensure that AC/DCs are as fair and objective as possible:
>
> - The possible inhibiting effect of being the only woman or individual from an ethnic minority group. The issue is particularly pertinent in interactive exercises such as a group discussion. The assessors may need to take this into account when evaluating the participant, but on the other hand, this could be a realistic situation. It is good practice to ensure that one of the assessors represents the minority group.
> - The relevance of the issues and scenarios of the exercises for all candidates. This is usually covered by careful design of the exercise.
> - The varying degree of experience that candidates have of participating in assessment programmes. This is usually covered by providing detailed briefing sessions or documents prior to the event.
> - The ability of the observers to judge participants against objective and job-relevant criteria, without allowing their own biases and stereotypes to influence them. This is usually covered by appropriate training of assessors in the skills of observing and evaluating behaviours, as well as by enhancing awareness of personal biases.
> - Any background circumstances which may affect a candidate's performance on exercises eg disabilities, first language. These factors should be taken account of when planning the assessment and interpreting the results.
> - Equal opportunities data should be monitored and the relevance of the skills and procedures regularly reviewed.

As you develop your approach, you will find that assimilating people with disabilities into your assessment procedures is less daunting and time-consuming than you might initially think. In addition, you may find that the presence of a disabled person actually enhances the team spirit. This is important in terms of transfer to the workplace!

ACCESS: ENABLING PEOPLE TO PARTICIPATE

Here is a list of points to consider in making your organization welcoming to people with disabilities. A more comprehensive account, including basic building regulations, can be found in Appendix 3.

Access for people using wheelchairs or with mobility difficulties

- Is there reserved parking for people with disabilities, adequately marked with the access symbol and close and accessible to the building entrance?
- Is the main reception accessible with wide doors on the ground floor, and is there a non-slip ramp, with adequate handrails?
- Are doors operable with minimum pressure?
- If access for people with disabilities is via a different entrance is this clearly signposted?
- Are there accessible toilets available?

Access for people who are deaf/hearing impaired

- Will a sign language interpreter need to be booked or will the applicant bring their own communicator? You will need to give an interpreter plenty of notice if you are planning to use one as they do get booked well in advance. You can find services listed in the Yellow Pages or contact the RNID (address and telephone number in Appendix 4).
- If the applicant wishes to communicate with you about the job or interview arrangements, a minicom number should be listed. If you do not have a minicom and your applicant is registered with Typetalk, you can use this service to link your company's voice service with the applicant's minicom system. E-mail might also be an option.
- Some applicants who are hard of hearing are happy to communicate using lip reading and their own voice. The applicant may feel that people sometimes take a few minutes to get used to their voice and request a pre-interview discussion. This is not unusual and if you have 10 minutes to give a short tour of your premises or discuss your company brochure, this ice-breaking exercise can be positive for both applicant and interviewer.

- Does the emergency evacuation system include both audible and visual alarms?

Access for applicants who are partially sighted or blind

- If an applicant is partially sighted, arrangements can be made to assist with the negotiation of your firm's layout.
- If information about your company is requested in Braille you can organize this by contacting the RNIB (see address list in Appendix 4).

Other additional needs

- Applicants may request regular drinks or a biscuit during an interview or assessment-centre type exercise.
- If an applicant is likely to have difficulty holding a cup, a straw can be available.

INTERVIEWS

Most disabled people will be able to cope with an interview on the same terms as their non-disabled counterparts. For the minority who cannot do so, it will be necessary to make arrangements to ensure that disabled applicants are able to demonstrate their suitability for the job for which they are applying. All candidates (not only those known to be disabled) should be asked if they have any individual requirements. Those who identify such a need might be offered an informal interview or telephone call to discuss this fully.

In particular, alternative forms of communication might be necessary at the interview. A deaf applicant might need a loop in the interview room, or an interpreter; a person with dyslexia or any other form of reading difficulty, or a speech difficulty, might need assistance perhaps in the form of extra time. Above all, the candidate should be asked how best his or her needs might be met. (For more details on preparing to interview people with disabilities, see Chapter 3.)

You may occasionally find that someone presents him or herself for interview without having informed you in advance of any disability. This is fine as long as the disability in itself does not affect the progress of the interview. But someone who has, for example, communication difficulties, is not actually acting very wisely if he or she turns up without having informed you and established any need for support at interview. No doubt the reason would have been largely about fear of being turned down by the company – in this case you would need to examine the extent to which your organization makes it clear to applicants that they will be fairly treated.

You would be better able to deal with a situation such as the above if you, as the interviewer, had had some training on disability issues. At least then you would feel more confident and comfortable in the interview. Your focus therefore could be on making the candidate feel at ease and in moving the interview along. If you are familiar with the most acceptable language to use (see Chapter 3) you will not hesitate in dealing directly and constructively with finding out about the candidate's abilities and the ways in which hiring him or her will benefit your team or organization.

Sometimes interviewers fight shy of addressing the subject of disability directly: they feel it is too personal or intrusive. If you are unsure, take the lead from the candidate. After all, that person in front of you will probably be quite used to living with a disability: it is part of him or her, just as wearing glasses is a part of many people's lives. You are quite justified in finding out whether the candidate has the skills and abilities to do the job, always bearing in mind the requirements of the DDA that you are prepared to make reasonable adjustments. So establish rapport, make sure you are aware of help available to you from outside sources such as the local disability employment advisers (for example, funding through the Access to Work scheme), and give the candidate every chance to demonstrate his or her suitability for the post. In addition, showing the candidate round the workplace can be a useful exercise for both of you, since you can then gather extra information about what adjustments you may need to make. Note also the DRT recommendations about enquiries that might be made at interview (page 65).

Terms and conditions of service

The duty of reasonable adjustment applies here too. It is permissible to offer a disabled employee a less favourable contract, but *only if* there is a material and substantial reason, and there is no possibility of making a reasonable adjustment to obviate this. For example, if you have made all possible arrangements to enable a person with a disability to perform in his or her job, and they still have a significantly lower output, that affects your business, you may pay him or her less.

Job Refusal Not Justified

Sandy v Hampshire Constabulary

Mr Sandy was registered disabled as a result of a back problem and partial loss of hearing. From November 1995, he was employed by Hampshire Constabulary over a period of 13.5 months as a station-enquiry officer on a series of temporary contracts. During this period, he had five days' sickness absence unrelated to his disability. In December 1995, he applied for a permanent station-enquiry officer position, was interviewed, and offered the job subject to medical clearance. He completed a medical questionnaire and supplied a medical report from his GP, stating that he did not 'anticipate any significant problems' in continuing to work on a permanent basis. However, the force's medical officer reported him unfit for work because of his back condition.

In his view, it would give rise to an unacceptably high level of absence. The offer of employment was withdrawn. Mr Sandy appealed against the decision and claimed unlawful discrimination. Subsequently, the medical officer reviewed his decision, having by then obtained Mr Sandy's attendance record. He reversed his recommendation and informed Hampshire Constabulary. However, by this time the vacancy had been filled.

A Southampton industrial tribunal (Chair: S J W Scott) held that Mr Sandy had been unlawfully discriminated against. The employer conceded that it had treated the applicant less favourably for a reason relating to his disability, but argued that the treatment was justified. The tribunal noted that the onus was on the employer to satisfy the tribunal that the decision not to employ was justified in the light of its knowledge at the time. In the tribunal's view, it could not be so justified. It found the medical officer's original decision that the applicant would need to take above-average sick leave to be 'arbitrary and speculative', since it was made without reference to his actual sickness record, conflicted with the GP's conclusion and was made without medical examination of the applicant. The tribunal stressed that the employer should not have relied solely on the recommendation of the force's medical officer but should have given consideration to holding the vacancy open pending the outcome of the applicant's appeal.

17 September 1997; case no. 3101118/97.

WELCOMING SOMEONE WITH A DISABILITY INTO YOUR TEAM

The extent to which it is advisable to prepare your team in advance will depend on the nature of the person's disability. You may wish to use the opportunity to put on some disability equality training, so that everyone's awareness is raised. Yet conversely it could be argued that it is not a good idea to make too big an issue of the disability, as it is the *whole person* who will need to feel welcomed for him or herself, rather than as the vehicle for a handy bit of awareness-raising.

Having offered a job to the disabled person, it is wise to ask him or her to visit you again to discuss any access issues (access in the widest sense, that is) that he or she can identify. At the same time you can ask about the best way to deal with the disability in terms of fitting into the team. You may find that some people would prefer it that colleagues are not informed of the disability, especially if it is not apparent. If that is how the person has successfully dealt with it in the past, then there may be no good reason to change. Some people with disabilities are happy to act as a role model or ambassador, spreading the word that disabled people are as capable as anyone else, but some are not comfortable with this. Take your cue from the individual in front of you.

Sometimes it can take a while to get the practical issues sorted out (eg raising or lowering work surfaces). Do bear in mind that the new employee will find it difficult to become totally integrated into the team if he or she does not have the tools for the job, so to speak. Sort everything out as quickly as possible, making full use of Access to Work funding (see Chapter 6) and advice from the Employment Service and other agencies.

Practical example: support while in post

Alison works in a merchant bank, in their IT department. She is blind and is enabled to stay at the forefront of technology because of the adaptations made to her workstation by the company she works for. She can access the e-mail system through a speech adapter on her computer, and reads printed documents using scanning equipment. Any training course handouts are put on tape for her, and the performance related appraisal system materials are available in Braille. Adaptations such as these are available to anyone with a disability who needs them: the organization's focus is not on the person's disability but on providing what is needed in terms of support to enable the employee to make the most productive possible contribution. In this way they were acting in the spirit of the DDA, even before its implementation.

CAREER DEVELOPMENT

Once assimilated into the organization, the person with a disability needs to be afforded the same chances as everyone else to manage and develop his or her career. Like all employees, he or she will need to be clear about your expectations, and that you appreciate openness and communication. You as the manager will have to find a way of giving support without removing responsibility. Using a mentoring system can be invaluable, as long as the mentor is properly trained.

Asking disabled people themselves to be mentors to new recruits is very empowering and gives a strong message to other employees about valuing the individual for what he or she can do, irrespective of disability. Consulting disabled employees about improvements to practice and policies is also highly recommended.

Any appraisal scheme you have in place will need to be flexible enough to cater for unexpected issues to do with disability, or diversity in general. An effective performance management system goes far beyond the once-yearly appraisal meeting: it identifies ways people can best contribute to their team, in the context of ongoing improvement and encouragement of initiative. Discussion of the impact of disability has a place in this, as long as you are able to handle it in a results-orientated way so that the person's self-esteem is enhanced and he or she feels empowered to continue to develop. Your mastery in delivering feedback, and your listening skills, will be crucial here. Using 360° feedback can be especially valuable in enabling a person to learn how best to progress.

National Vocational Qualifications

If your organization is committed to the national drive towards the National Learning Targets, and in particular to encouraging employees to gain National Vocational Qualifications (NVQs), you should be aware that special arrangements, if necessary, can be made for assessment of candidates with disabilities. As you may know, there is a complex hierarchy of different bodies and individuals involved in the delivery of these qualifications, from the QCA and from many National Training Organizations who are responsible for setting the standards, through the awarding bodies down to the thousands of centres where assessment takes place. Your organization might in fact be such a centre.

In the case of verified schemes, ie NVQs, GNVQs (General National Vocational Qualifications) and other schemes involving ongoing assessment which accredit competence against specified criteria, candidates may use mechanical, electronic or other aids to demonstrate their competence as long as the aids are generally commercially available and can be feasibly used on employers' premises. In other words, if an employee manages his or her job by using special aids, then competence can be assessed in the same way, even though that special aid would not normally be used by non-disabled candidates. Further, whereas awarding bodies normally only certificate a *unit* of competence as the smallest portion of an NVQ, in the case of a candidate who cannot complete a whole unit because of disability, certification of an *element* of competence is possible.

In the case of GNVQs, where an external test is required, special arrangements may be made as with other examinations. These include an allowance for extra time, the use of an amanuensis or reader, the use of a signer in some cases, or Braille question papers for blind candidates. In all cases, NVQs and GNVQs, the special arrangements are strictly monitored, and there is no question of standards being altered for disabled candidates. They, like everyone else, must reach the required level of competence.

Further information about NVQs and GNVQs and special arrangements is on page 115.

Practical example: career development

Sometimes one can be too eager!

A course leader was presented with a difficulty as a result of a decision to distribute Braille handouts to a participant in advance of the course taking place. The other participants were given the handouts on the day in the usual way, and so were much less prepared than the blind person, who subsequently revelled in the extra knowledge and power, subverting some of the processes designed into the course!

SICKNESS ABSENCE

Managing this can be extremely difficult. A golden rule is to document everything that you do. The following two case studies illustrate different aspects of this issue.

Sick-pay Change Justified

O'Dea v Bonart Ltd

Over a three-year period up to December 1996, Mr O'Dea, who was registered disabled because of a leg injury suffered in a road accident, had taken 107 days' sickness leave. Under guidelines in his contract of employment, he was eligible for three months' sick pay per year – two on full pay and one on half pay. When the company learned in December that he would have to have a further four months off sick for an operation, it wrote to him saying that the guidelines in his contract did not apply and that any sick pay given would be at management's discretion. An Exeter industrial tribunal (Chair: B E Walton) found that the unfavourable treatment on grounds of disability was justified.

> In our judgment the letter could constitute unfavourable treatment under s.5(1) (a) but the respondents were entitled to be concerned in this particular case about the length of time he was finding it necessary to have off work ... The implication in the letter is that he will not actually receive sick pay for the forthcoming period of absence, but that is a matter which in the circumstances could be justified as a proper exercise of the respondents' discretion having regard to the amount of sick pay the applicant has received over the years.

10 April 1997; case no. 1700168/97.

Over £12,000 Awarded In DDA Claim

Howden v Capital Copiers (Edinburgh) Ltd

An Edinburgh industrial tribunal (Chair: A Bolland) holds that an employee who had frequent sickness absence because of abdominal pains was dismissed by reason of his disability and awards £12,659 compensation.

The applicant was employed as a stock controller from 5 December 1994 to 13 December 1996. He suffered from abdominal pains suggestive of ureteric colic, though there was no exact diagnosis. Between November 1994 and April 1997 he had been admitted to hospital on six occasions and had been operated on in May 1996 and October 1996. Without effective pain control, he was unable to walk, experienced a severe gripping pain, had to lie down, lost the use of his hands, was doubled up, suffered spasms, lack of coordination, speech impediment, blurred speech, loss of concentration and manual dexterity. Following 35½ days' sickness absence during 1996, he was dismissed without warning.

Rejecting the employer's submission that the applicant was not disabled in terms of the Disability Discrimination Act, the industrial tribunal held that the dismissal was unlawful disability discrimination. It found that the abdominal pain was a 'physical impairment notwithstanding the absence of an exact diagnosis', which had a substantial adverse effect on his ability to carry out normal day-to-day activities, and, given that the condition had lasted for more than two years, was long term. Accepting the applicant's submissions, the tribunal took the view that the applicant had been discriminated against by being treated less favourably than others would have been treated who did not have the applicant's condition, because he had been dismissed for absence due to illness in circumstances where someone acting frivolously would have been warned. It awarded compensation of £12,659, including £1,000 for injury to feelings.

30 July 1997; case no. S/400005/97.

It is best that you keep abreast of current case law on this issue. We suggest that you take expert legal advice before acting in any individual's case and remember that it is helpful to distinguish between disability and incapability.

RETENTION: EMPLOYEES WHO BECOME DISABLED

People already employed by your organization at the onset or worsening of their disability are also covered by the DDA, so you need to do all you can to enable them to continue working for you. From a financial point of view alone, this makes sense: recruiting and retraining new staff could be far more costly than making adjustments to enable the person already doing the job to remain in it.

A comprehensive equal opportunities policy in the company will make provision for employees who become disabled. The conditions for such situations will need to be set down in a suitable document such as a staff handbook. Whatever is laid down in procedures will work best if there are arrangements to consult the individual person and draw up a timetable with him or her. When, as will often be the case, the person has had a period of sick leave, the timetable will need to include specific points of contact, a visit to the former workplace, and a briefing for the absent worker. In only a short time there are likely to have been changes in systems, people and products. A period of positive rehabilitation leave might be beneficial. Some organizations are setting up disability leave schemes to cater for this need, or developing intervention strategies with specialist insurance companies.

75

Reasonable Adjustment Duty Satisfied

Wood v Darron Motors Ltd

Laurence Wood was employed as a motor mechanic. In October 1995, he was involved in a motor accident which resulted in the loss of his right leg below the knee. He returned to work the following April, initially part-time and then full-time, but only at 60 per cent to 70 per cent capacity. As well as adjusting his working hours, the employer also spread his workload and generally accommodated him with time off. However, following problems with the amputation, Mr Wood was absent from work from November. The employer met with him and obtained medical reports on his condition. In February 1997, it was decided to dismiss him as there was no certainty of a return to full-time work in the near future and there was no alternative work for him. He claimed disability discrimination.

A Southampton industrial tribunal (Chair: L W Belcher) dismissed the claim. It held that the applicant had not been treated less favourably than any other employee who had long-term illness and faced future absences. It accepted that the duty of reasonable adjustment applies to employees already in work, but found that during the six-month period when the applicant returned to work, the employer carried out the required adjustments in accordance with s.6. It also found that had the applicant continued his employment,

> it would not have been unreasonable for the respondents to have said that they could not comply with s.6 on a long-term basis and that it would have been reasonable for them to have set up the justification under s.6(4) in regard to the financial and other costs.

11 August 1997; case no. 3101084/97.

When the disabled person is ready to return to work, your options for them can include the following, taken from Employment Service (1993):

- returning to the same job;
- redesigning job content or working methods;
- changing working hours or place of work;
- equipment or workplace adaptations;
- some retraining to find new ways to use old skills;
- other jobs within the organization;
- using work experience to try out new ideas;
- organizing a gradual re-entry to the job to build confidence and make sure all the arrangements are working efficiently.

You can use the Employment Service to help assess the best ways to use people's abilities. The local Disability Employment Advisor (DEA) will possibly arrange a referral to the Disability Service Team's occupational psychologist or other specialist. After retraining, the person's redeployment will need to involve a wide range of people, including co-workers. You may find that people are quite shocked to see a former friend return, perhaps looking or acting differently as a result of their disablement. They, too, will need empathic handling.

Interestingly, the Institute for Employment Studies survey, *Employers' Attitudes to People with Disabilities*, found the following to be true:

> Even among organisations which did not employ people with disabilities, attitudes towards the retention of existing employees who become disabled are considerably more positive than those towards the employment of people with disabilities in general.

Practical examples: becoming disabled while in employment

Alan was acting supervisor of the production shift at the plant of a manufacturing company when an explosion occurred. He was totally blinded. A long period of adjustment followed, including two stays at the Royal National Institute for the Blind rehabilitation centre at Torquay. Alan was reluctant to go away for a long period of training such as is provided at the RNIB college at Loughborough, because he had just remarried. An interest in computers, identified at Torquay, was developed in his home area.

The company were keen to reintegrate Alan into their workforce, although by then he had moved home away from the area in which the factory was situated. Over a long period, the company, the RNIB, the Disability Employment Adviser and Alan developed a resettlement plan which was accepted by all concerned. Alan would be located on the site of another factory owned by the group, but would still be working for a senior manager at the manufacturer's headquarters. Alan's new job is that of computer analyst.

Dave was a forklift driver at a large distribution centre. He slipped on a dirty warehouse floor, severely fracturing an arm, which resulted in continuous pain and lack of grip.

He was transferred to the goods inward office until a newly appointed manager decided he was not going to have light duties workers in his department.

Dave still has no job, and the company is facing recruitment problems, health and safety questions, unfair dismissal proceedings, and a substantial claim for damages, including loss of earnings.

SELECTION FOR REDUNDANCY

It is essential to make sure that any decisions you make can be proven to be justified. This can be difficult sometimes, but the following case study shows how enormous compensation awards can be made against employers who use disability as a way of making someone redundant.

£103,000 Disability Award

Kirker v British Sugar plc

A Nottingham industrial tribunal (Chair: D R Sneath) holds that a visually-impaired chemist selected for redundancy was discriminated against on grounds of disability and awards compensation of £103,000.

Nicholas Kirker, whose vision is so poor that he is eligible for full blind registration, was employed as a shift chemist at British Sugar's Newark plant until he was made redundant in March 1997. He scored 40.5 points out of a possible 100 under the redundancy selection criteria; the lowest score of those who succeeded in retaining their jobs was 46. He claimed that he had been discriminated against contrary to the Disability Discrimination Act (DDA) and unfairly dismissed.

Upholding his claims, the tribunal found that his score for certain individual criteria reflected a wholly subjective view of him, the origins of which lay in his disability. He scored 0 out of 10 for 'performance and competence', yet was never criticized for poor performance or lack of competence. He also scored 0 out of 5 for 'potential', with management viewing his disability as a health and safety problem. Points were also deducted for absenteeism, yet the reason for his absence related to his disability. In the tribunal's view, an objective assessment which was not influenced by the disability would have produced average scores, taking him well above the 'quality line'.

The tribunal awarded compensation of £103,146.* It awarded past loss under both the DDA and the Employment Rights Act (£7,167); the rest, the bulk of which was for future loss, was awarded under the DDA only. Taking account of evidence showing that visually-impaired people face huge barriers in securing employment, the tribunal based its calculation of future loss on the assumption that Mr Kirker would not find alternative employment for the rest of his working life (15 years), reduced by 20 per cent for the risk that had he remained in employment his eyesight would have deteriorated to such an extent that he would have been unable to perform his duties. It also awarded £3,500 for injury to feelings.

*Note that this was later raised to £167,000 when it was found to be taxable.

5 December 1997 and 9 January 1998; case no. 2601249/97.

The EAT dismissed an appeal by British Sugar.

HEALTH AND SAFETY

This is often one of the main areas of concern for employers, particularly if they are unused to working with people with disabilities. In fact, their worries are often unjustified, as the Institute for Employment Studies survey showed. This quotes the example of the Royal Mail in Merseyside which, with the financial help of the Employment Service, had considered fitting flashing lights to fire alarms. It was also planned to designate certain members of staff as responsible for letting deaf people know in case of an emergency. In practice deaf people simply followed other people when the drill sounded! This anecdote is not designed to encourage you to be complacent about your existing practices, merely to urge you to use a healthy measure of common sense when thinking about disability.

However, there are certainly circumstances which would make it dangerous for people with particular disabilities to carry out certain work. The following case study illustrates the various points of view in such a case. Note the roles of the doctors in this!

Suspension Of Employee With Epilepsy Not Unlawful

Smith v Carpets International UK plc

Mr Smith, who had epilepsy, was employed as a warehouse operative in February 1994 by Carpets International UK plc. He was seen by the company doctor in February 1996. He explained that he had had one or two dizzy spells in the last two years, but that he had not had a full-blown epileptic fit for nine years. The doctor concluded that Mr Smith's epilepsy was controlled and decided not to impose any restrictions on his working. However, there followed a number of reports of Mr Smith having epileptic seizures and he was examined once again by the company doctor in

November. The doctor concluded that it was dangerous for Mr Smith to work in the warehouse because of the significant amount of heavy machinery and fork-lift activity. He recommended that Mr Smith be suspended until his epilepsy became controlled. A risk assessment was carried out which concluded that no adjustments could be made to the warehouse work. Mr Smith was suspended on sick pay. In February 1997, Mr Smith's consultant reported that he was fit to return to work, and he did so in March. However, the company doctor disagreed with the consultant's view, especially as the consultant had never visited the workplace and was not aware of the specific health and safety dangers. He once again recommended suspension from work. An offer of alternative work was made but Mr Smith was unwilling to accept it as it would have meant a significant drop in pay. The employer conceded that it had treated Mr Smith less favourably because of his disability by subjecting him to a detriment but relied on the defence of justification.

A Leeds industrial tribunal (Chair: J M Hepworth) upheld the defence. In its view, the applicant's treatment, 'because of the important health and safety reasons, was justified because the reasons for it were clearly material and substantial'. It added that the employer 'had carried out reasonable investigations as to what adjustments could possibly be made to accommodate' Mr Smith. However, taking 'into account the questions of practicability and financial cost', the tribunal took the view that it was 'not reasonable to expect the respondent to do what would have amounted . . . to a total change in the way in which the respondent carried out its work. The respondent could not reasonably be expected to have made arrangements which removed fork-lift trucks from the warehouse, for example. They did, however, offer the applicant a different place of work . . . The steps were ones which the tribunal found to come within s.6(3).'

11 September 1997; case no. 1800507/97.

DISMISSAL

Over half the complaints received through the UK employment tribunal system concern dismissal. Many of these cases will be linked to claims of unfair dismissal, enabling employment tribunals to make a reinstatement order under the unfair dismissal legislation, if appropriate, together with uncapped compensation. (Employment tribunal applications under the DDA may cover more than one complaint. For that reason, the number of actual applications lodged will be lower than the number of complaints.) These case studies show how the tribunals are dealing with this difficult question.

Forklift-Truck Driver's Dismissal Unlawful

Hardy v Gower Furniture Ltd

Mr Hardy, one of two forklift-truck drivers in the company's raw materials department, was employed from February 1988 to March 1997, when his employment was terminated. He is registered disabled and had various disabilities by way of asthma, heart conditions, back injuries which prevented lifting and the loss of parts of certain fingers. He went on sick leave on 9 January 1996, returning on 17 January 1997. During that time a replacement forklift-truck driver had been employed. Following Mr Hardy's return, the company carried out a redundancy exercise among the three drivers. Because of his disabilities, Mr Hardy scored the lowest on the redundancy criteria. The company offered alternative employment which it knew he could not do because of his disabilities, and made him redundant when he rejected them. A Leeds industrial tribunal (Chair: D J Latham) held that he had been unlawfully discriminated against. In its view:

> [if Mr Hardy had not been disabled,] he would not have had his employment terminated, as he would not have been selected for dismissal. The respondents cannot ... argue that they kept the two other forklift-truck drivers and only offered alternative employment that the applicant could not conceivably carry out or accept, and then maintain that the applicant was not less favourably treated.

29 July 1997; case no. 1802093/97.

MS Dismissal Not Justified

Samuels v Wesleyan Assurance Society

Mr Samuels, a salesperson with the Wesleyan Assurance Society, was absent on sick leave for a month in April/May 1996, and was further absent from September until his dismissal in December. At the end of September, Mr Samuels's neurologist indicated that he had multiple sclerosis (MS). The neurologist wrote to the employer in November stating that he did not see any major objection to Mr Samuels returning to work and that it might be a question of 'trying and seeing'. Notwithstanding this opinion, and Mr Samuels's intention to return at the end of certified absence in January, he was dismissed. He successfully claimed breach of the DDA. A Liverpool industrial tribunal (Chair: D Reed), finding that Mr Samuels was a disabled person for the purposes of the Act, rejected the employer's claim that his less favourable treatment was justified. Mr Samuels had expressed a firm intention to return in a very short time and the Society would only be paying statutory sick pay to him in the interim. In the tribunal's view there was no reason why the employer could not 'try and see' as the neurologist had suggested. It accepted that some costs might be incurred in bringing Mr Samuels 'fully up to speed' on developments that had occurred during his absence, but they would not 'be on anything like the scale that might justify the Society in dismissing Mr Samuels, even given the possibility of less-than-perfect attendance on his part'.

23 July 1997; case no. 2100703/97.

PROACTIVE DISABILITY MANAGEMENT AT WORK

It is certainly the case that, both in the US and in the UK, employers are increasingly looking at ways of managing disability as part of their overall 'wellness' programmes. These can be seen as having three levels:

1. Broad programmes, aimed at the total workforce, eg lifestyle, stress management etc.
2. Targeted programmes aimed at particular conditions which may be related to the nature of the work, eg back pain management or prevention.
3. Specific programmes such as would be useful to individuals with long durations of disability.

In particular, the avoidance or containment of depression that often accompanies the experience of becoming disabled, as well as being a potential disability on its own, is crucial but complex. One of the best alleviators is prompt action, based on communication and support.

In the US, the profession of rehabilitation counselling is well established. In the UK, this is not yet the case; we have to fall back on generic skills that exist in the workplace, for example in occupational health. But if the process of disability management is seen as a collaborative one in which the employer acts swiftly and competently, it will benefit the individual, who will continue to feel valued, and also the organization, as costs will be minimized and litigation will become less likely.

An excellent resource pack for employers, employees and their representatives is produced by RNIB, and is called *Get Back* (visit www.rnib.org.uk or telephone 0845 702 3153). It covers various disabilities and offers excellent suggestions, presented in a simple way, for helping in the process of returning to work.

INSURANCE MATTERS

It is becoming increasingly common for employees who are off work due to long-term illness or disability to have an entitlement to some kind of insurance payment. Employers will be familiar with the various forms of private health insurance. The most relevant of these are income protection policies which replace income when one is unable to work due to illness. About half of these are actually funded by employers, mainly for more senior employees. The other half are funded by the employees themselves, who usually comprise higher level earners.

The major insurers and re-insurers are now becoming more conscious of the need to take positive action to ensure a return to work as soon as possible (as in the US). They are investing in their own rehabilitation systems or buying in services to assist this process. One leading re-insurer, Swiss Re, is to coordinate a consortium of 17 firms. Working in collaboration with the Employment Service's 'New Deal' programme (see page 117) in which beneficiaries (volunteers only, initially) are invited to see a personal adviser to discuss return-to-work strategies. Other firms employ their own rehabilitation counsellors – often nurses with an occupational health background or occupational therapists – to visit absent employees, suggest rehabilitation and initiate steps for a return to work.

The insurance firms' approach is based on what they believe to be good commercial sense; this is shown in the following analysis:

Why is there an interest in rehabilitation from income protection insurers?

Because:

- the benefit is paid when the claimant is unable to work;
- the benefit is income related, not flat rate;
- 15,000 claims are in force at any one time;
- benefits encourage recipients to settle into a retired lifestyle;
- there are financial savings to be made by returning more people to work and doing this quickly.

How does it work?

1. Referral by insurer (claims manager) for assessment.
2. Telephone assessment by rehabilitation professional (occupational therapist or occupational health nurse).
3. On-site case conference with employer.
4. Physical rehabilitation, retraining, job adaptation, rearrangement of work etc.
5. Return to work.

Benefits to insurer

- reduction in claims or duration of claims;
- reduction in premiums;
- more business.

The effect of these practices on employers can only be beneficial, and there would be much to be gained by collaborating with insurers who operate them.

A NOTE ON COSTS

It is often asked whether there are any additional costs associated with the employment of disabled people. Sometimes there are, but more generally there are no direct costs at all: disabled people take their place in the workforce on the same terms as anyone else, and if they and their jobs have been carefully matched they do so without being a financial drain on the employer. In a few cases, in which aids or adaptations or other special support facilities are needed, there are some costs, but a recent government survey of its Access to Work scheme showed them to be small, ie less than £300. Exceptionally, they are greater. Large or small, many of the costs are absorbed by the Access to Work scheme.

On the broader front of employers' reservations about the recruitment of disabled people, Honey et al (1993) found that extra costs were rarely seen as a concern, with fewer than 1 per cent of the survey's respondents reporting this reservation.

There will of course be some indirect costs which will vary according to the size of the firm and how much effort is put into its equal opportunities policies and practices. If you have no written policy at present, it might cost anything up to £2,000 in administrative costs (and more for subsequent dissemination and training) for large organizations who instigate a formal policy as a result of the new legislation: less of course if you only need to adjust an existing policy. (For further analysis, see Department for Education and Employment, Social Analysis and Research Division, November 1995, *Compliance Cost Assessment: Analysis of familiarisation costs of the Disability Discrimination Act*, included in consultation pack, 1996.)

Perhaps a more important area to look at is the cost of *not* managing disability issues properly! Employees who take prolonged sick leave, perhaps because they cannot see how to manage the disability themselves and have no help from their employers, will incur far more expense than an employee who works *with* a manager to contain the problem and sort out reasonable adjustments. Also, litigation is much more likely to be initiated by employees dissatisfied with their managers' approach than by those who feel supported and valued.

SOME MORE IDEAS . . .

Have you considered taking on disabled people for work experience? This can benefit both sides: you will be able to find out what it is like working alongside someone with a disability, and the individual will be able to gain valuable experience to add to his or her CV or portfolio – and neither side is permanently committed to anything! On the other hand, you may well find that you are able to recruit a good worker as a result, at minimum cost to yourself.

People come forward for work experience often when they are at school or university. They are a valuable conduit for messages you wish to spread about your organization's approach to diversity – so use them! You might wish, for example, to ask them to write something on their experience for your in-house magazine.

In order to make work experience placements successful for both the employer and the person with a disability, it is important that both parties are clear about their joint objectives. The following points, taken from the former Surrey CEPD (Committee on Employment of People with Disabilities), should be taken into consideration when arranging work experience placements:

- Good planning – meet with the school or Employment Service representative and the person with a disability beforehand to discuss the placement.
- Set out clearly the company's needs, the job and the tasks involved in the form of a job description or contract.
- Agree a work programme for the individual for the period of the placement, including any review procedures.
- Arrange for a named member of staff to supervise the placee's work.
- Arrange for any necessary facilities to enable the individual to carry out the tasks associated with the job, if appropriate.
- Carry out a review of the person's placement at the end.
- Provide a written reference for the placee.

The Job Introduction Scheme allows you to take a disabled person on to your staff for an initial period of 6 weeks (extendable to 13 weeks) during which time you can both assess the person's suitability for the post. It must be a genuine full- or part-time job, which is expected to last for at least six months after the trial period ends. You can get help towards the person's wages for the first few weeks: he or she will be paid the normal rate for the job. If you are interested in this scheme, contact the disability employment adviser at the Jobcentre (see also Chapter 6).

Practical example: work experience

A major supermarket chain has an established work experience programme for undergraduates. Following aptitude tests and an interview, students are placed for eight weeks in the summer after their second year at university, and given significant projects to do. Michael, a partially sighted student who undertook such a period of work experience, found to his delight that the organization was not interested in his impairment, only in where his strengths lay. People in the department where he worked were keen to treat him as an individual and meet his needs (eg for enlarged print) so that he could be free to do his best in the job. This attitude in turn enhanced his motivation and commitment, and reinforced his view that as a disabled person it is important to take responsibility for asking for whatever you need. The company's readiness to respond to this resulted in their forming a relationship with a highly motivated and ambitious individual, who would prove to be a loyal employee in the organization. After the summer placement, Michael was awarded a scholarship to help him through his final year at university. A year or two on, he knows that his disability has taken second place to his obvious strengths and creativity, and he is now permanently and productively employed by the company.

SEEKING ADVICE FROM OUTSIDE

There are many potential sources of help. Some useful organizations are listed in Appendix 4 and, in Chapter 6, you will find details of the role of the local disability employment adviser, whom you can contact through the Jobcentre. He or she will be able to advise you on the following:

- practical advice on putting the symbol commitments into practice;
- a speedy response to vacancies (in partnership with the Jobcentre) to help you recruit someone with a disability;
- access to expert guidance if an employee becomes disabled;
- advice and individual help to get specialist equipment or adapt the work environment if necessary;
- information on all the available sources of help.

KEEPING UP THE GOOD WORK: MONITORING PROGRESS

Being involved in diversity initiatives is exciting: you get a real feeling of possibilities opening up before your very eyes! The problem perhaps comes in maintaining this momentum. But, as with many aspects of management, the ongoing results are what count. This means that you need to have a clear system of monitoring and evaluating your progress towards your stated goals. For the purposes of defending yourselves at an employment tribunal against possible compensation claims with regard to discrimination, you need to keep up-to-date records on policies and practices. Use and review these regularly, on a consultative basis, with the aim of having a rolling programme of improvements in diversity management.

CHECKLIST: CHAPTER 4

1. Do your advertisements positively welcome people with disabilities?

2. Are they placed where disabled people are most likely to see them?

3. Is the job/person specification limited to relevant criteria?

4. Do you interview all qualified disabled people and, if so, have you publicized this fact?

5. Do you ask all applicants if they have any particular needs for interview and for work?

6. Is the interview/testing plan checked for suitability?

7. Are additional facilities for interview provided for people who need them?

8. Are you familiar with the help available and the agencies who can provide it?

9. Have your staff involved in recruitment had up-to-date disability awareness training?

10. Do you move swiftly to help an employee who is off work?

11. Do you regularly seek legal advice?

12. Do you document everything?

5

Policies and codes

PUTTING IT ALL INTO PRACTICE: PLANS FOR ACTION

We recognize that not everyone who is reading this book will be part of an organization with an explicit equal opportunities or diversity policy, statement or code of practice. We have found that this is often true of small- or medium-sized enterprises. For this reason, Chapter 5 looks at suggested items for inclusion in such a policy, with some contacts and examples to provide you with some inspiration.

THE NATIONAL APPROACH: SUGGESTIONS FROM THE GOVERNMENT

Over the years, a number of codes of practice have been produced, and most recently, the *Code of Practice for the Elimination of Discrimination in the Field of Employment against Disabled Persons or Persons who have had a Disability* (The Stationery Office, 1996) has been published for the Government. This is dealt with more fully in Part 2, Chapter 7.

A forerunner of the new code, the *Code of Practice on the Employment of Disabled People* (Employment Service, 1984) is now out of date because of the recent legislative changes. However, it still provides useful material for local codes or in-house policy statements and action plans. Much of the information included in the code is similar to that given in the earlier chapters of this book: for example, ensuring that job requirements are strictly related to the needs of the job, and assisting employees who become disabled to retain the jobs they already have or to be redeployed in more suitable work within the organization. Two sections are worthy of being quoted in full since they suggest some very sound objectives and establish a framework for ensuring that all aspects of disability equality action are coordinated at senior level.

Suggested objectives for companies in employing people with disabilities

- The company should be recognized by the community as one which provides good employment opportunities to people with disabilities.
- People with disabilities who apply for jobs with the company should know that they will receive fair treatment and be considered solely on their ability to do the job.
- The company should have a policy for looking after employees who became disabled and the norm should be to retain them in suitable employment.
- People with disabilities who join the company or employees who become disabled should be integrated smoothly into work and any special needs they may have concerning work or the working environment should be examined thoroughly.
- The company should develop the skills and potential of disabled employees to the full and offer them training and promotion opportunities according to their abilities.
- All employees in the company should accept disabled colleagues as readily as able-bodied colleagues. [Author's note: 'non-disabled' is preferable to 'able-bodied'.]
- The company should ensure that it is meeting its legal obligations towards employing people with disabilities.

Co-ordinating your Policy and Practice towards Workers with Disabilities

There are many areas to consider in relation to policy and practice towards workers with disabilities. Some companies, particularly large ones with an established personnel function, may therefore find it helpful to nominate an executive to co-ordinate all matters affecting disabled people's employment and to be responsible for developing positive and constructive practices at all levels in the company.

The duties appropriate to this post might include:

- involvement with policy development on the employment of people with disabilities;
- making arrangements for all managers, employees, including employees with disabilities, and their representatives to be involved in developing policy;

- encouraging all managers, supervisors and employees in the implementation of good practice and ensuring that appropriate information and training about disability are provided;
- monitoring all aspects of policy to check that it is being implemented, including in the following areas: recruitment, induction, training and career development of employees.

The effectiveness of a policy will often turn on the extent to which it is owned by all concerned. Therefore it is best developed in consultation with them and in particular with disabled employees and disability groups in the community who will always have a valuable contribution to offer.

THE EMPLOYERS' FORUM ON DISABILITY

Matching the efforts of Government at national level have been those of the Employers' Forum on Disability. The Forum is a not-for-profit company funded by its several hundred members who include many of the major national names in business. Its aim is to enhance the economic prospects of disabled people by making it easier for employers to employ and serve them. The Forum:

- promotes information exchange across industry and commerce about best corporate practice;
- provides a networking and publications service;
- promotes communication and partnership between employers, disabled people, service providers and government;
- encourages government and voluntary sector agencies to develop policies and services which reflect employer expectations and requirements;
- represents employers in policy debates.

The address is in Appendix 4.

The Forum's Employers' Agenda on Disability

A concise representation of the Forum's approach is set out in its ten-point plan as follows:

1. **Equal Opportunities Policy and Procedures Statement**
   The employment of people with disabilities will form an integral part of all equal opportunities policies and practices.

2. **Staff Training and Disability Awareness**
   The company will take specific steps to raise awareness of

disability throughout the organization, particularly targeting all staff involved in recruitment and selection processes.

3. The Working Environment

The company will take all reasonable steps to ensure that the working environment does not prevent disabled people from taking up positions for which they are suitably qualified.

4. Recruitment

The company will review and develop recruitment procedures which encourage application from and the employment of people with disabilities.

5. Career Development

The company will take specific steps to ensure that disabled people have the same opportunity as other staff to develop their full potential within the organization.

6. Retention, Retraining and Redeployment

Any employees who become disabled will be given the fullest support to maintain or to return to a role appropriate to their experience and abilities within the company.

7. Training and Work Experience

The company will ensure that disabled people are involved in work-experience, training and education/industry links.

8. People with Disabilities in the Wider Community

The company will recognize and respond to disabled people as customers, suppliers, shareholders and members of the community at large.

9. Involvement of Disabled People

When implementing the ten points for action, the company will encourage the participation of disabled employees to ensure that, wherever possible, employment practices recognize and meet their needs.

10. Monitoring Performance

The company will monitor its progress in implementing the key points. There will be an annual audit of performance reviewed at board level. Achievements and objectives will be published to employees and in the UK annual report.

LOCAL POLICY AND PRACTICE NETWORKS

Below national level there are many local or organization-specific codes of practice which reflect to a greater or lesser degree the principles of the national ones. In case readers want to make contact, it is worth mentioning the Milton Keynes and North Bucks Disability Employment Network which, like the Employers Forum, has published its own *Disability Action File*. Similar networks can be found in Birmingham, Huddersfield, Fife, Hampshire, Northern Ireland and Reading (addresses can be found in Appendix 4). There may well be others: check with your DEA for local information.

In our research for this book we came across many organizations with valuable codes and policy statements, action plans and similar documents that again reflect the principles set out in this book. Most are quite lengthy but included at the end of this chapter is that of the Open University which provides a very readable and comprehensive example.

POLICY STATEMENTS

Because of the length of full codes of practice, it is useful to try to encapsulate the main principles in a succinct policy statement which can be widely publicized inside and outside the organization. Unfortunately it is often the case that in striving to be concise, writers neglect the special requirements of disability. One employer who managed to combine brevity with adequate representation of disability was Midland Bank plc (now HSBC Bank).

Midland Bank PLC
Equal Opportunities Policy

- We seek to employ a workforce which reflects the diverse community at large, because we value the individual contribution of people, irrespective of sex, age, marital status, disability, sexuality, race, colour, religion, ethnic or national origin.
- We will treat all Midland employees with dignity and respect and we will provide a working environment free from unlawful discrimination, victimisation or harassment on the grounds of sex, age, marital status, disability, sexuality, race, colour, religion, ethnic or national origin.
- We will not tolerate acts which breach this policy and all instances of such behaviour, or alleged behaviour, will be taken seriously, be fully investigated and may be subject to the Bank's disciplinary procedures.

- We will make every effort, if an existing employee becomes disabled, to retain them within the workforce, wherever reasonable and practicable.
- We will install facilities for people with disabilities in existing premises, whenever practicable to do so. Whenever we invest capital in new or refurbished premises, every practical effort will be made to provide for the needs of staff and customers with disabilities.
- We will provide banking products and services to our customers and clients without any form of unlawful discrimination.

Considering all the issues, we suggest that there are some basic and unavoidable criteria that must be taken into account: these are summarized below.

Developing an equal opportunities policy statement to include reference to disability

The statement might include the following key points as a basic minimum:

- Disability should be explicitly mentioned.
- The emphasis is on relevant criteria only for selection.
- A positive image should be portrayed.
- Employees who become disabled in service will be retained in suitable positions wherever possible.
- The policy will be operated in consultation with wide representation, including disabled people.
- The statement should take account of current legislation.
- Disability awareness training will be provided at all relevant points in the organization.

Publicizing the statement and reviewing it

It is of little use having a statement if no one sees it. You might therefore consider where and how your statement or a part of it should be publicized. All company literature could be considered for this and all company venues, eg staff notice boards, might display it. It is also necessary to ensure that the policy is reviewed from time to time. An annual audit might be carried out or commissioned to facilitate such a review.

Model equal opportunities policy statement

A suggestion for a model equal opportunities policy, including disability, might be on the following lines:

The organization recognizes that direct and indirect discrimination might take place and therefore sees the need for a positive and effective equal opportunities policy.

We will promote the concept of equality of opportunity throughout the organization. In particular, we will ensure that:

- in recruitment and selection, candidates will be assessed against relevant criteria only, ie skills, qualifications and experience;
- all employees have equal chances of training, career development and promotion;
- the policy is developed in consultation with a wide range of representation covering the whole workforce and the community;
- the language used in documents will reflect and promote equal opportunities;
- the policy is reviewed and evaluated periodically, and improved and developed as appropriate.

Practical steps that will be taken include the following:

- venues for meetings will take account of the needs of all participants;
- access to documentation will include alternative formats such as tape, disk and large print;
- all staff, and in particular those concerned with selection and promotion, will be given equality awareness training;
- job specifications will make a reference to equal opportunities;
- application forms for jobs will include a question about equal opportunities – or interview questions will do so, for example, how will the applicant contribute to the policy?
- people with disabilities will be offered facilities at interviews to enable them to demonstrate their suitability for employment;
- people becoming disabled while in employment will be given positive help to retain their jobs or be considered for redeployment if that is necessary;
- all recruits to the organization will be offered induction which will include a reference to the organization's equal opportunities policy;
- a senior member of the organization will have personal responsibility for the equal opportunities policy.

EQUAL OPPORTUNITIES WITHIN A WIDER CONTEXT

Over recent years there have been a number of developments in the human resources field that reflect the increasing acceptance of policies which develop all of all people's potential (see our discussion of diversity as a concept in Chapter 2).

The message here is that if your company or organization is applying for Investors in People status, or any similar kitemarking initiative, or if its managers are following continuing professional development (CPD) programmes, it would be a good idea for the principles set out in this book, in keeping with the spirit of the DDA, to be incorporated in some way into those developments. The material in this book is intended to contribute to the body of knowledge on the specific subject of its title, but more particularly to help managers ensure that they are familiar with the issues.

AN EXAMPLE OF AN EFFECTIVE CODE OF PRACTICE

The Open University

Code of Good Practice on the Employment of Disabled People
This Code has been produced by the Open University Disability Advisory Team.

1. MISSION
It is University policy to extend and develop opportunities for disabled people to work on equal terms. The University recognises that disabled people are seriously under-represented in its workforce and is committed to greater participation through the development of equal opportunities measures.

2. INTRODUCTION
The aim of this Code is to develop a working environment which will ensure that disabled people are selected solely on the basis of their merits and abilities. As part of the University's commitment to equal opportunities a Code of Good Practice on the employment of Disabled People was developed in 1991/92. This code, which is subject to regular review, takes into account the requirements of the Disability Discrimination Act 1995. The Code aims to assist managers in the provision of employment opportunities for disabled people at all levels within the University and create a working environment where disabled

staff do not experience barriers to full participation in the life of the University. Much of what is contained in this Code reflects good equal opportunities practice. It specifically addresses the issues relating to disability as this group of staff are under-represented in the University's workforce.

3. LEGISLATION

The Disability Discrimination Act received Royal Assent in November 1995. The employment provisions of the Act began to take effect from the end of 1996.

The employment provisions of the Act apply to employers who employ more than 15 people.

The Act applies to disabled people who have, or have had, a disability which makes it difficult for them to carry out normal day to day activities. The disability could be physical, sensory, or mental. It must also be substantial and have a long-term effect, i.e. it must last or be expected to last for 12 months. Conditions which have a slight effect on day to day activities, but are expected to become substantial, are covered. Severe disfigurement is also classed as a disability.

Employers will have to take reasonable measures to make sure they are not discriminating against disabled people.

It is unlawful for an employer to treat a disabled person less favourably than someone else because of their disability, unless there is a justifiable reason. This applies to all employment matters including recruitment, training, promotion and dismissal.

Employers have a duty to look at what changes they could make to the work place, or to the way work is done, which would overcome the effects of the disability, and make any changes which are reasonable. Until relevant case law is established it may be difficult to interpret what 'reasonable changes' actually means in real terms. It is clear that the interpretation of this will vary with the size of the employer. However, the Government have issued a 'Code of Practice' which gives advice and a copy of this has been sent to all Heads of Units and Sub Units.

Disabled people who feel an employer has discriminated against them can complain to an Employment Tribunal. They could also ask the Advisory Conciliation and Arbitration Service (ACAS), or in Northern Ireland the Labour Relations Agency (LRA), to help them to settle the complaint without an employment tribunal hearing where possible.

The Registration and Quota Scheme has ended. Disabled people no longer need to register and employers are no longer required to employ a set quota of registered disabled people.

The Disability Rights Commission Act 1999 received Royal Assent on 27th July 1999. The main aim of the Act is to establish a Disability Rights Commission, which will work towards the elimination of discrimination against disabled people. The Commission will: promote the equalisation of opportunities for disabled people; keep the Disability Discrimination Act under review; assist disabled people by offering information, advice and support in taking cases forward; provide information and advice to employers and service providers; undertake formal investigations; prepare statutory codes of practice providing practical guidance on how to comply with the law; and arrange independent conciliation between service providers and disabled people in the area of access to goods and services. It is intended that the Commission will be set up during the year 2000.

Further information on the Disability Discrimination Act can be obtained from the **Disability Advisory Team** (details of membership of the team can be found at the end of this code).

4. THE OPEN UNIVERSITY AIMS:
   i.   To promote a positive working climate so that disabled people are readily accepted within the organisation.
   ii. To examine the work environment and practices in order that disabled staff do not experience barriers to their full participation in the life of the University.
   iii. To ensure the development of the skills and potential of disabled staff, according to their abilities, through staff development and promotion opportunities.

5. OBJECTIVES:
   i.   To ensure that disabled applicants receive full and fair treatment and are considered solely on their ability to do the job.
   ii.   To compose job descriptions, person specifications and advertisements which do not include unnecessary restrictions. Careful consideration should be given to the actual requirements of the job.
   iii. To provide applicants with the opportunity to have further particulars in alternative formats such as large print, on disk, in braille or on tape.
   iv.   To design advertisements to encourage disabled applicants.
   v.   To develop specific strategies to widen awareness of job vacancies.
   vi.   To interview all disabled applicants whose skills and experience meet the 'essential' criteria of the person specification.
   vii. To retain staff who become disabled in their current role wherever possible, or to find a suitable alternative role if available, and provide retraining where necessary.
   viii. To provide induction and support for all disabled members of staff.

ix. To ensure that, where practicable, all new and existing University buildings, whether offices or study centres, are accessible and comply with the Disability Discrimination Act and other legislation.

6. RECRUITMENT AND SELECTION

The employment provisions of the Disability Discrimination Act apply to all aspects of the recruitment and selection processes. You are strongly advised to read the 'Code of Practice for the elimination of discrimination in the field of employment against disabled persons or persons who have had a disability' before starting the recruitment process. A copy of this document was sent to Heads of Units and Sub-Units in November 1996. Additional copies can be purchased from HMSO Publications Centre.

The following should also be read in conjunction with 'Good Selection Practice: A Guide for Interviewers' (which is available from the Personnel Division, Personnel Services Section).

6.1 *Job Description and Person Specification*
The inclusion of unnecessary or marginal requirements in a job description or person specification can lead to discrimination.

Flexibility is required in considering both the job and the way in which it can be carried out. Imposing unnecessarily rigid requirements for jobs may exclude many suitable candidates, and can disproportionately affect disabled people. Job descriptions and person specifications should therefore be assessed and drawn up in as flexible a way as possible.

Care should be taken to be specific in explaining the essential duties required of the applicant. Some examples follow:

i. 'Ability to communicate' is too vague and should be expressed in terms of the actual tasks that require verbal/written communication skills. Where the use of a telephone is essential an estimate of the amount of time and type of use should be indicated.

ii. Requiring applicants to possess a driving licence which immediately excludes non-drivers. Instead some indication of the amount and type of travel required should be indicated.

iii. Stipulating that applicants should be 'energetic' when the job is largely sedentary in nature, could unjustifiable exclude some people whose disabilities result in them getting tired more easily than others.

iv. Stating that applicants must have a certain level of educational qualification when this is not necessary in order to do the job, could discriminate against someone who has a learning disability, which has prevented them from obtaining that qualification.

NB: Where a disabled person enquires about a post, but for reasons of their disability could not carry out a small percentage of the job duties, they should not be discouraged from applying. The provisions of the Disability Discrimination Act require that employers consider making a reasonable adjustment to the role to accommodate a disability (see also shortlisting section).

6.2 *Advertising*

i. Advertisements should only ask for skills and abilities needed for acceptable job performance (as with job descriptions and person specifications).

ii. A name should be included in all advertisements of someone who can be contacted within the department for information on access. Applicants asking for information in alternative formats will also be referred to that person.

iii. All advertisements placed by Personnel will be circulated to the Milton Keynes Disability Employment Adviser. Advertisements placed by Regional Centres should be sent by the Regions to the appropriate local Disability Employment Adviser.

iv. All advertisements should carry the statements, 'Disabled applicants whose skills and experience meet the requirements of the job will be interviewed' (see shortlisting section for further clarification), and 'Please let us know if you need your copy of the further particulars in large print, on computer disk, or on audio cassette tape. Applicants who are deaf or hard of hearing may make enquiries on Milton Keynes (01908) 654901 (Minicom answerphone). Equal Opportunity is University Policy'.

v. The University will on a regular basis place promotional advertisements regarding employment opportunities in selected disability publications.

6.3 *Further Particulars*

i. Further particulars provide an ideal opportunity to inform applicants about aspects of the post which are additional to the advertisement. Further particulars should include a prose version of the essential duties contained in the person specification and a statement that the University welcomes applications from disabled people. They should also indicate why it is helpful to know about the individual needs of an applicant who might be called to interview and specific detail about the physical environment in which the person will be required to work. Further particulars should be made available in alternative formats such as large print, braille, on tape or on disk. Help and advice can be obtained from **Derek Child, Assistant Director in the Equal Opportunities Team**. The information given in the further particulars should seek to encourage and widen participation and reassure applicants that information requested on the application form is sought in an attempt to make selection a fairer process.

ii. The application form states that 'The Open University welcomes applications from disabled people, and information about disability is only requested in order that appropriate arrangements for an interview can be made if necessary'. This should be repeated in the further particulars.

iii. Shortlisted applicants should be sent a copy of the Access Guide to the Walton Hall campus which gives details of car parking, accessible routes for wheelchair users and the location of adapted toilets and lift access. This map is also available in tactile form for blind and partially sighted visitors. **For copies of the map, contact the Communications Group, ext. 52938**.

6.4 *Shortlisting*

All disabled applicants who meet the essential criteria of the person specification must be interviewed. In cases where a disabled person does not meet the selection criteria, the employer is still under a legal duty to consider if the disabled person would meet the criteria with a 'reasonable adjustment'. Until there is some established case law in this area, it is difficult to assess what would be considered to be a reasonable adjustment. Consideration must be given to the practicality of taking measures to reduce any obstacle which places the disabled person at a substantial disadvantage. Adjustments may include:

- making adjustments to premises;
- allocating some of the duties to another person;
- altering hours of work;
- acquiring or modifying equipment;
- modifying instructions or reference manuals;
- modifying procedures for testing or assessment;
- providing a reader or interpreter;
- providing supervision.

Written reasons for not interviewing a disabled applicant will be required as part of the normal process of recording selection decisions for all vacancies. See 'Good Selection Practice A Guide for Interviewers'. If you have any doubts or concerns with regard to the shortlisting of disabled candidates, please discuss these with the **Personnel Officer in the relevant team in the Personnel Services Section of the Personnel Division**.

Assumptions should never be made concerning a person's capabilities. There are numerous types of equipment and other aids to assist disabled people in the workplace where these are required. The list is extensive and continually growing. In most cases the disabled person themselves will be aware of any equipment available, alternatively contact the **Personnel Officer in the Directorate Section of the Personnel Division**.

Many disabled applicants will require few, or no, adjustments in order to carry out the duties of a job.

6.5 *Interviews*
   i.   It is University policy that all staff involved in the selection process undergo formal training by the University which includes an Equal Opportunities element. It is essential that the interviewing panel are familiar with the provisions of the Disability Discrimination Act 1995.
   ii. Standard interview procedures can be followed but in certain circumstances specific arrangements will be necessary e.g. physical access to buildings, car parking arrangements, sign language interpreters etc. Invitation to interview letters must ask whether candidates have any individual requirements for the interview.
   iii. The ability of a candidate to undertake the duties of the job will be the only consideration. This point should be made to the candidate at the beginning of the interview.
   iv. If the applicant has indicated that they have a disability it is mandatory that this be raised at interview. In all respects the format of interview should be the same for all candidates, however, after the formal questions have been asked the issue of the applicant's disability should be raised. Failure to raise the issue at the interview, could result in an assumption that the University has failed to address the issue and has therefore discriminated against the individual.

The Disability Discrimination Act requires an employer to make reasonable adjustments to the work place and working practices in order that a disabled person can carry out the role if they are the most suitable candidate.

It is suggested that the following question is asked at interview to cover this issue:

"We have explained the duties of the role. You have indicated on your form that you have a disability. Can you tell us if there are any adjustments that you feel would need to be made in order for you to perform the role, should you be successful?"

101

It is important to remember that it is up to the University to make the decision as to what reasonable adjustments should and could be made, in many cases the adjustments will be minor. As well as the individual advising of any adjustments they feel might be necessary, it would be advisable to contact your relevant Personnel Officer in Personnel Services who can advise on this. In some cases special equipment may be required, and in this case the Personnel Officer can contact relevant organisations for advice, and in some cases, financial support.

The applicant's answer concerning the above question should not be taken into account in deciding whether or not they should be appointed to the post, unless you are able to provide very good reasons as to why the adjustments which need to be made are not reasonable. These reasons should be discussed with the Personnel Officer in your Personnel Services Team.

v. If a disabled person shortlisted for interview is not offered the job, the Chair of the Appointment Committee should set out in writing the reasons for the decision as is standard recruitment practice for all unsuccessful applicants within the University.

7. JOB REGISTER

A job register, containing names and details of disabled applicants seeking employment in the Milton Keynes area, will be maintained by Personnel. All external advertisements will be provided to applicants from the Register by the Personnel Division. Potential applicants may discuss general access, and any other issues with a member of the Personnel Division.

8. INDUCTION, TRAINING AND CONTINUING SUPPORT

As the University develops, individuals' roles and work will change. Training and induction programmes should be made available to recognise and support these changes. These programmes should be accessible to all staff.

The Line Manager will be responsible for discussing with disabled appointees their individual needs such as particular equipment, car parking etc., and then ensuring that this support is provided. Advice is available from the **Disability Advisory Team, and from the Occupational Health Department** who can arrange to undertake ergonomic workplace visits and advice on equipment if necessary.

Confidentiality should be maintained at all times and the appointee, in consultation with the Line Manager, should decide what information concerning their disability or the support they require is divulged to their colleagues. Any issues relating to individual training needs should be discussed with the **Training Officer of your Personnel Services Team**.

It is recommended that an existing member of the office should act as a temporary guide/mentor to offer assistance if necessary to the new employee. As well as the mentor, the new employee should be given the name of the Line Manager and of members of the Disability Advisory Team to whom they can go for advice or assistance.

9. RESOURCES

The University will use all means of assistance both advisory and financial including the Employment Service's Disability Services Team (formerly known as PACT), the Disability Employment Adviser and the local Job Centre. Contact and liaison with other specialist organisations and networks including the Milton Keynes and North Bucks Disability Employment Network and the Employers Forum on Disability will be fostered.

The Disability Advisory Team have produced a resource pack on disability awareness. Your recruitment co-ordinator will have a copy of this (or telephone the Personnel Division, extension 52849 for further information).

The Access to Work Scheme: Disabled people are entitled to a range of different services under the scheme including interpreter support, personal reading support, aids and equipment, adaptations to property and equipment and fares to work. The University will be expected to meet part of the cost of these provisions for employees, other than those newly appointed who have been unemployed for 4 weeks or more. Full details of this Scheme can be obtained from the **Personnel Division**. Managers and supervisors will be advised of the range of practical and advisory assistance available from the various organisations who can assist with employment, recruitment and placement. Specialist advice and support relating to particular recruitment/redeployment situations will be available from the **Personnel Division**.

10. WORK EXPERIENCE

The University will, in collaboration with other specialist organisations, offer work experience placements to disabled people, where appropriate.

11. DISABILITY REHABILITATION

Disability rehabilitation is available for staff who become disabled during the course of their employment with the University. The primary aim is to enable staff to retain and return to their former job and/or be found suitable alternative employment within the University.

The Disability Discrimination Act requires employers to make reasonable adjustments to the work and workplace, to resolve any difficulties which arise as a result of an employee becoming disabled. Reasonable adjustments may include those detailed in the shortlisting section of this document, and/or additional training where appropriate. Staff will be given the opportunity to discuss their expectations, anxieties and wishes including financial and other relevant specialist advice on a planned basis with their Line Manager and Personnel Division. Confidential advice is available from the **Occupational Health Department**, which may also be involved in advising on tasks and work equipment.

12. ACCESS

The Estates Division is committed to making all University buildings and sites accessible through its Minor and Major Works Programme, where reasonable, but recognising there are considerable difficulties with some established University sites. The University already meets the statutory access requirement laid down for new buildings. Where buildings such as Regional Centres are relocated the access needs of the potential staff/student user of leased office accommodation must be considered. Where property is leased the Act modifies the effect of the lease so far as necessary to enable the employer to make alterations if the landlord consents, and to provide that the landlord must not withhold consent unreasonably.

Staff responsible for negotiating sites and locations for residential schools and study centres should endeavour to follow the University's Policy of providing an accessible environment for both study and work.

Staff requiring guidance on specific adaptations or planned minor works should contact the **Estates Division**. A map and access guide indicating routes to buildings, lift access, toilets and reserved parking at Walton Hall is available on request from **The Communications Group**. For access information on other University sites, contact should be made direct.

13. HEALTH AND SAFETY

Particular attention will be paid to any individual health and safety issues relating to disabled employees to ensure that they and their colleagues are fully aware of the safety procedures to follow in the case of an emergency.

Department Safety and/or Fire Officers will be familiar with the different methods of evacuation for disabled employees particularly those who are wheelchair users. In all cases individual staff will be consulted about their individual needs for evacuating their building in a safe and dignified manner, in advance of any emergency, ie. as part of risk assessment.

The needs of staff who are deaf or hard of hearing or those who have visual impairments will be recognised with particular reference to light alarms and procedures to follow where other human assistance may not be available.

Unit Heads and/or Line Managers should ensure that a risk assessment is carried out in accordance with the Open University Health and Safety Policy. **Contact Health and Safety Section (Ext. 53344)** for information or advice.

14. INFRINGEMENT OF THE CODE

The University as an employer is responsible under the Disability Discrimination Act to ensure that its staff involved in selection and other relevant employment issues are adequately informed and trained in relation to disability issues. However, staff involved in such activities also have a personal responsibility to ensure that the guidelines as outlined in this code and the Government 'Code of Practice' are followed. Individual Managers as well as the Open University as an employer may be liable to compensatory claims under the provisions of the Act. In addition to any legal claims which may arise under the Act, the University will decide on appropriate action to be taken, depending on the individual circumstances.

15. DISABILITY ADVISORY TEAM

Further advice and support on the implementation of this Code can be sought from members of the Disability Advisory Team, who will call on other specialist support as necessary:

Richard Burton, Estates Division	Extn. 53276
Carolyn Buckby, Personnel Officer, Personnel Services	Extn. 53067
Derek Child, Assistant Director, Equal Opportunities Team, QA&R	Extn. 52867
Jez Grzeda, Business Manager, KMI	Extn. 55761
Janet Shine, Staff Development Adviser, Personnel Division	Extn. 54051
Dawn Steel, Personnel Officer, Personnel Division	Extn. 52849
Christine Tennent, Assistant Director, Personnel Division	Extn. 53668

Team members updated November 1999

* Guidance Notes for staff dealing with access enquiries from Disabled Applicants

Query	*Contact person for staff handling enquiry*
1. Further particulars in alternative formats: e.g. large print, Braille, disk, tape	Derek Child, Assistant Director, E.O. Team ☎ 52867 will be able either to arrange this or advise the appropriate contact.

2. Physical Access

Factual information should be provided on ramps and availability of lifts etc. Further information on the feasibility of adaptation to premises to meet an individual need is available from Richard Burton in the Estates Division, ☎ 53276.

Access map showing ramps, lifts, toilets for disabled staff, parking etc., at Walton Hall is available from Diane Seymour in the Communications Group ☎ 52936.

3. Individual needs e.g. flashing lights (for people who are deaf or hard of hearing) braille numbers, adaptations to toilet facilities etc.

Advice available from Richard Burton in the Estates Division ☎ 53276.

4. Individual equipment needs

Dawn Steel (Personnel Officer) Personnel ☎ 52849.

5. Individual support required to facilitate interview procedure e.g. lip speaker, signer

Information available from the Personnel Officer in your Personnel Services Team: Hazel Jenner/Simone Russell ☎ 53345 Jenny Barrett ☎ 52203 Carolyn Buckby ☎ 53067

* Staff in Regional Centres may wish to consult their Recruitment Co-ordinator in the first instance.

With acknowledgements to the Open University.

To contact the main switchboard of the Open University, call: 01908 274 066.

CHECKLIST: CHAPTER 5

1. Does your organization have a code of practice on equal opportunities or diversity?

2. Does it have a succinct policy statement?

3. What is the place of disability within these?

4. Do your codes and policies cover all the areas suggested in this chapter?

5. Are disabled people fully involved in the development and monitoring of the effectiveness of your code and policy on equal opportunities or diversity?

6

Sources of support

Research projects and surveys consistently report that misconceptions and lack of awareness contribute significantly to the high rates and duration of unemployment among disabled people. In the qualitative follow-up study (Thomas, 1992) to the *Employment and Handicap Survey* (Prescott-Clarke, 1990) it was found that there remained a considerable need to increase employers' and employees' awareness and understanding of:

- the workplace implications of disability;
- the need for flexible working arrangements;
- the system of adaptations and grants available through the Employment Service;
- the availability of professional advice and help.

Although nearly ten years have passed, the situation is much the same. In this chapter we list the main sources of support and suggestions about the employment of disabled people. It is convenient to group these forms of help into three main categories:

1. statutory services;
2. voluntary sector services;
3. employer networks.

Appendix 4 contains an expanded list of useful contacts and addresses.

STATUTORY HELP

Disability Service Teams

The Employment Service has Disability Service Teams to provide an advisory service for employers and people with disabilities. Disability employment advisers (DEAs) mentioned earlier are members of the teams and are usually located at Jobcentres.

Specialist services for disabled people

Disability employment advisers can provide:

- initial employment/needs assessment;
- referral if appropriate to work preparation, occupational health assessment and/or ergonomic assessment;
- in-depth job-seeking advice;
- information on and referral to specialist Employment Service programmes for disabled people, including Access to Work, the Job Introduction Scheme and the Supported Employment Programme (details below);
- referral to training;
- provision of ongoing support.

Specialist services for employers

DEAs also provide specialist help and advice to employers to support them in adopting good employment policies and practices in the recruitment, retention, training and career development of disabled people. They can visit employers and advise them about the practical and financial help available, including adaptations to premises or the provision of special aids to employment under the Access to Work Programme. Advice may also be provided on the disability symbol, which has been developed so that employers can show their commitment to good practice in the employment and retention of disabled people.

Services provided include:

- advice if there are practical points to consider when employing someone with a disability:
- a speedy response to vacancies (in partnership with the Jobcentre) and help to contact suitable disabled people;
- advice on the work environment;
- help with developing good practice within an organization;

- guidance on the Job Introduction Scheme (see below) if a disabled person is recruited for a trial period;
- advice on Access to Work (see below) and the funding available;
- help in assessing the best way for newly-disabled employees to continue using their skills and experience at work;
- financial help to employ someone with a more severe disability, if there are places available under the Supported Employment Programme (see below);
- information on other sources of specialist help;
- continuing support after a company has recruited someone with a disability and while it implements new policies.

See page 117 for information about 'New Deal'.

Access to Work

Access to Work provides funding and other help for people who have a disability to help them enter or stay in employment, including self-employment, on an equal footing with non-disabled people by removing obstacles that exist because of the disability. It applies to any job, part- or full-time, permanent or temporary.

How Access to Work can be used

The programme has a variety of possible applications: for example, Access to Work can help pay for:

- a communicator for employees who are deaf or have a hearing impairment (this includes having a communicator at a job interview);
- a part-time reader or assistant at work for people who have a visual impairment;
- a support worker (who may be an existing employee) for someone who needs practical help, either at work or getting to work;
- adaptations to equipment or new equipment to meet individual needs;
- alterations to premises or a working environment;
- adaptations to a car, help towards taxi fares or other transport costs if a disabled employee cannot use public transport to get to work.

These are just some examples of ways in which Access to Work can be used when you employ someone with a disability. If you identify other possibilities, it is worth discussing these with the DEA and your employee or potential new recruit.

The DEA can meet you and your job candidate or employee, and can visit the workplace to discuss the best approach. Options available could include simple adjustments to the work environment or office equipment, or structural changes to make buildings more accessible.

Access to Work funding

Access to Work pays for *all* the approved costs of support for:

- people in self-employment;
- travel to work;
- communicator support at interview;
- people who have been in their job for less than six weeks, or are about to start a new job.

For people working for an employer who have been in their job for six weeks or longer, the programme meets up to 80 per cent of approved costs above a threshold of £300 and below a ceiling of £10,000, and 100 per cent of approved costs above £10,000, over a three year period.

Supported Employment Programme

The Supported Employment Programme provides employment for over 22,000 disabled people, who, because of the nature or effects of their disability, have difficulty in securing and retaining work without practical or financial support to them or their employer, but who are able to make an effective contribution to the employing organization or company. A key value of the programme is its ability to tailor support to the individual and provide him or her with the opportunity to reach his or her potential, offering long-term support where needed and help to progress to open employment if possible.

If you would like to know more about the Supported Employment Programme, you should contact the DEA at your local Jobcentre.

Job Introduction Scheme

The Job Introduction Scheme (JIS) offers employers a weekly grant of £75 towards the cost of providing a trial period of employment for a disabled person if the employer has doubts about the person's ability to cope with the job or working environment. The trial normally lasts for six weeks, but can be extended to thirteen if doubts remain. JIS is aimed at disabled people who are ready to enter open employment. It is administered by DEAs, is simple for employers to apply for and is delivered quickly.

The trial must be for a paid job expected to last at least six months after the end of the trial period, and can be used for part- and full-time work with any employer with the exception of government departments and agencies. It cannot be used in supported employment.

Help in attracting people with disabilities

Becoming a disability symbol user

The purpose of the disability symbol is to help employers show that they welcome disabled people as employees, and to help disabled people identify employers who have a positive attitude towards their abilities.

The five commitments that symbol-users agree to implement cover recruitment, development and retention of employees with a disability, awareness-raising with key employees and monitoring progress and improvements. The commitments are to:

1. Interview all applicants with a disability who meet the minimum criteria for a job vacancy and consider them on their abilities.
2. Ensure that there is a mechanism in place to discuss with disabled employees at any time – but at least once a year – what you can both do to make sure they are able to develop and use their abilities.
3. Make every effort when employees become disabled to make sure they stay in employment.
4. Take action to ensure that all employees develop the appropriate level of awareness needed to make your commitments work.
5. Review these commitments each year, assess what has been achieved, plan ways to improve on them and let all employees and the Employment Service know about your progress and plans.

Putting these commitments into place will provide a firm focus for your current and potential disabled employees to know what you expect from them – and what they can look for from you and your organization. If you want to use the symbol, you should contact your local DEA.

The Employment Service's Disability Service provides information about their programmes and services in a range of formats, including: leaflets; audiotapes; Braille and a British Sign Language (BSL) subtitled video. These should be available from your local Jobcentre, but if you experience any difficulty in obtaining them, please contact the Employment Service on 0114 259 6427 and relevant copies will be sent to you.

VOLUNTARY SECTOR HELP

There are many organizations in the voluntary sector that are concerned with disability; the major national organizations that have a significant role in employment matters are listed in Appendix 4. These will offer advice at the very least, and some of them will have very specific employment roles that might be of use to you. These include:

Royal National Institute for the Blind: an extensive employment service, including technical advice on aids and adaptations for blind and partially sighted people and other means of access to employment and information about work and training and retraining.

Scope (formerly the Spastics Society): a fast track management training scheme for graduates with disabilities.

Workable is involved in several employer networks, and also operates a graduate support scheme, placing disabled graduates into work experience placements, short or long term.

Blind in Business: specific help in matching blind and partially sighted people with job opportunities in business.

Mencap: a wide range of services relevant to employment and in particular *Pathway*, a job placement scheme for people with learning difficulties.

In addition, many of the organizations concerned with other specific disabilities eg cystic fibrosis, diabetes, haemophilia, while not offering an employment service as such, publish information relevant to the implications of the disability in holding a job.

The above are the main sources of help at national level. There will be many at regional level which can be identified locally but if you have any difficulty then it might be useful to go through RADAR (Royal Association for Disability and Rehabilitation) which, apart from having an extensive role in employment, training and education, is in touch with hundreds of local associations.

EMPLOYER NETWORKS

The Employers' Forum on Disability is the only major national body of its kind, and offers many opportunities for cross-fertilization of ideas. Details are given in Chapter 5.

There are many local networks, for example the Milton Keynes and North Bucks Disability Employment Network. This is a prime example of local employers coming together to discuss relevant issues and to create a forum which can carry out practical work (publishing the *Disability Action File*, for instance) and influence service providers and policy makers if that is what they wish to do. A list of local employer networks on disability is given in Appendix 4.

If you have any difficulty in finding out if there is a relevant local body, and if so where it is, the best thing is to contact one of the major national bodies such as Workable (see Appendix 4). If there is no local network, somebody might be inspired to start one.

SCHEMES AND INITIATIVES

This group of schemes comprises those which are not specifically for disabled people, but disabled people, like anyone else, might take part in them. It is therefore important for readers to know of their existence, though this book is not the right place to go into great detail about them. The following brief summaries might be helpful.

Advanced Modern Apprenticeships are government-funded employer-led, work-based training packages for young people, which lead to NVQ/SVQ Level 3 or above. They are available in most sectors of industry and help to meet the demand identified by employers, for a new high quality route to meet changing skill requirements at craft, technician and junior management level. In most cases, the trainee will have employed status, but exceptionally will be on a training allowance. The apprenticeships are not timebound, the time taken being dependent on the needs and abilities of the young person. Employers choose their recruits from young people under 25 not taking part in any other government-funded scheme and not attending college full time. The government wishes to encourage into the scheme more people with disabilities, who are currently under-represented. A study *Modern Apprenticeships and People with Disabilities* is available from the DfEE.

National Traineeships (Foundation Modern Apprenticeships) are similar in purpose and structure, except that they are geared to the needs of young people aiming at NVQ/SVQ Level 2.

NVQs, **SVQs** and **GNVQs** are relatively new qualifications. NVQs and SVQs are qualifications based on competence – the ability to perform a job to standards laid down by industry. They are available in 11 different occupational fields and reflect the skills, knowledge and understanding that people have in relation to specific areas of work within those fields. They:

- conform to standards laid down by employers – in effect, the NTOs (National Training Organizations) which are the lead bodies for particular sectors;
- are open to anyone; there are no time limits, age limits or entry requirements;
- enable learning to be done in any way, at any place, and over any period of time, with as many attempts as are necessary;
- take account of skills the learner already possesses;
- are made up of units of competence which can be gained one by one, or altogether, as appropriate;
- all have five levels numbered one to five, covering basic work activities to senior management/professional level;
- include the key skills of communication, numeracy, information technology, working with others, improving your learning and performance and problem solving.

GNVQs (General National Vocational Qualifications) are related to broad areas of work, but unlike NVQs/SVQs, provide a *general* education as a preparation for employment of further study. Generally speaking, they are only taken by young people in schools and colleges, as an alternative to GCSEs or A Levels. Advanced GNVQs are renamed 'vocational A Levels' under curriculum 2000, which modernizes the post-16 provision.

People with disabilities who wish to achieve any of the above qualifications may take advantage of additional help if they need it, though there is no question of lowering the standards. For example, a visually impaired person might need to be provided with material in Braille or large print, a hearing impaired person might need a signer and interpreter and/or amplified speech, while people with all kinds of disabilities could benefit from extra examination time or the help of an amanuensis. Guidance is available as to the most suitable form of help, but two general principles are that the help should be similar to that which the candidate has had during his or her learning, and any devices used should also be capable of being used in future employment.

For some disabled people, mainly those with learning difficulties, the standards in the qualifications already discussed might be too demanding. As a result of recommendations in the report by Dearing on 16–19 provision, a new entry level qualification is being developed. Most of the major examining and awarding bodies (see next paragraph) already had an award of this kind available, but they were not regarded as part of the NVQ Framework. They are now being reviewed to ensure that they meet the criteria laid down by the DfEE and the QCA (Qualifications and Curriculum Authority) (also see next paragraph) such as progression to a higher qualification.

With regard to GNVQs and special help that might be needed, the Joint Council of National Vocational Awarding Bodies publish a booklet: *Assessment in General National Vocational Qualifications – Provision for candidates with particular requirements (special assessment needs)* (revised annually). For GCSEs, similar guidance is available and the individual awarding bodies publish their own (OCR, 1999). All vocational qualifications were overseen by the National Council for Vocational Qualifications (NCVQ) until 1 October 1997 when the responsibilities were transferred, with those of the Schools Curriculum and Assessment Authority (SCAA) to the new body: Qualifications and Curriculum Authority (QCA).

The awards are made by the relevant awarding body for the sector and/or the well known awarding bodies like City and Guilds. In the case of GNVQs, awards are only made by Edexcel, City and Guilds, and OCR (Oxford, Cambridge and RSA Examinations). Edexcel was created by the merger of BTEC (Business and Technology Education Council), and London Examinations, while City and Guilds of London Institute has become part of an alliance (Assessment and Qualifications Alliance) with AEB (Associated Examining Board) and NEAB (Northern Examinations and Assessment Board). RSA Examinations Board has joined forces with UCLES (University of Cambridge Local Examinations Syndicate) to become the OCR (Oxford, Cambridge and RSA Examinations).

National Record of Achievement (NRA) is, as the name suggests, a document used to bring together details of a young person's experiences and attainments throughout the latter years of education and into working life. It is issued before he or she leaves compulsory education. In addition, it is available to be used as a planning document to help the owner consider his or her future development and make plans and arrangements to obtain further skills and qualifications. Finally, it may be used as a presentation portfolio to show to employers when applying for a job, so that the interviewer gets a full picture of the applicant and his or her abilities and potential. Later, it might form the basis of discussions about in-service training and development.

The NRA was first issued in 1991, and it is now being reviewed. The Dearing Report on the Review of Qualifications for 16- to 19-year-olds, while recognizing its value, recommended a review, restructuring and relaunch. Trials and market testing have taken place and a new version will be phased in, possibly from 2000. The name 'Progress File' has been used as a working title.

The NRA can be especially useful for people with disabilities, since their educational and work experience records are often different. Their schooling might have been interrupted for treatment, for example, and they might not have been able to get even the work experience from Saturday jobs that many students value. The NRA will show ways in which they have developed, and how they bring certain qualities, not available to others.

New Deal is a cornerstone of the Government's pledge to get people off benefits and into jobs. This is intended to bring advantages not only to the participants but to employers and the whole economy. The scheme started by catering for young people in pathfinder areas in January 1998 and became a nationwide provision in April 1998, and was later extended to older people and other groups. Employers can play a significant part in the scheme, by:

- offering young people jobs through New Deal, which give them the chance to show what they have to offer and contribute;
- taking the opportunity to help make their businesses or organizations more successful and profitable by drawing on this key source of potential recruits.

People with disabilities may participate in New Deal and they will not need to have been unemployed for the normal period to enter. In addition to the mainstream facilities however, a budget has been set aside for certain projects to develop a personal advisor service, and to look at innovative ways of helping more severely disabled people and long-term sick people to enter paid employment.

Further Information

For more information about any of the above Schemes and Initiatives, approach your local Training and Enterprise Council (TEC) or local chamber of commerce, except in the case of New Deal which operates through the Employment Service, so contact the local Jobcentre.

It should be noted, however, that TECs are likely to be superseded in this regard by Learning and Skills Councils from 1 April 2001. The new councils will be responsible for funding all training and for the education of 16- to 19-year-olds and adult learning (though not work-based learning, which will move from the TECs to the Employment Service). Higher education funding will remain the responsibility of the English, Scottish and Welsh Funding Councils.

DISABILITY CONSULTING GROUPS

These are gatherings of people with expertise and influence who offer practical support to the Disability Service Teams. They include employers, employee representatives, disabled people and members of voluntary organizations, and meet once or twice a year for briefings and an overview of developments. Contact will be through the local DEA or Jobcentre.

ACDET (ADVISORY COMMITTEE FOR DISABLED PEOPLE IN EMPLOYMENT AND TRAINING)

At national level, ACDET is sponsored by the DfEE and advises ministers and officials on:

- Securing equality of participation in employment, self-employment and training opportunities for disabled people, in particular, those with significant impairment.
- Recruitment, promotion and retention of disabled employees and support services covering their employment, self-employment, careers advice and training.
- Research programmes and services.
- The effectiveness of DfEE-funded labour-market interventions for helping disabled people.

PART 2

LEGISLATIVE CHANGES

A SUMMARY

The Disability Discrimination Act 1995 (DDA) received Royal Assent on 8 November 1995 and came into force for employment and some other purposes on 2 December 1996. It is described in the statute in the following words:

> An Act to make it unlawful to discriminate against disabled persons in connection with employment, the provision of goods, facilities and services, or the disposal or management of premises; to make provision about the employment of disabled persons; and to establish a National Disability Council.

For employment purposes, the Act, in a nutshell, makes it unlawful for an employer of 15 (originally 20) or more people to discriminate against a disabled person, either in considering whether to offer employment, or in the treatment of that person when employed, including the taking of decisions about whether to retain or dismiss them. Discrimination means that an employer must not treat any employee or job applicant less favourably, because of a reason relating to his or her disability, than other people to whom that reason doesn't apply, including other disabled people, unless that treatment can be justified.

The Disability Rights Commission Act 1999 provides for the setting up of the Disability Rights Commission (DRC). This will strengthen the enforcement of the DDA since many of the powers of the DRC are similar to those of the Equal Opportunities Commission and the Commission for Racial Equality. The Commission began operating in April 2000. The following commissioners were appointed:

Bert Massie (Chair)
John Hougham (Deputy Chair)
Saghir Alam
Kay Allen
Jane Campbell
Michael Devenney
Richard Ewing
Kevin Fitzpatrick
Peter Humphrey
Colin Low
Elaine Noad
Evelyne Rank-Retruzzietto
Philippa Russell
James Strachan
Jenny White

7

Employment provisions of the DDA

INTRODUCTION

The employment part of the Disability Discrimination Act (DDA) applies to employers of 15 or more people. Those who employ fewer than 15 are exempt. The employment provisions do not apply to people serving in the armed forces, police officers, fire fighters, prison officers and prisoner custody officers or anyone employed on board ships, hovercraft or aeroplanes, nor to those who work wholly or largely outside Great Britain.

Employers are still able to recruit or promote the best person for the job. They are not expected to make any changes which would break health and safety laws.

It is now unlawful for an employer to treat a disabled person less favourably than someone else because of their disability, unless there is good reason. This applies to all employment matters including recruitment, retention, training, promotion, transfers and dismissal. It is also against the law for employers' associations, trade unions and certain professional bodies to discriminate against a disabled person.

To help a disabled person do a job, employers must also make any reasonable changes to the workplace or work methods. In considering what is reasonable, they will be able to take into account the costs of changes and how much they would help. Disabled people who feel that they have been discriminated against may complain to an employment tribunal. They may also seek the help and support of the Disability Rights Commission (see page 152).

All the duties covering employers were introduced on 2 December 1996. A Code of Practice for the elimination of discrimination in employment was published in the summer of 1996. This is not itself a statute but it may be used in consideration of complaints to tribunals who are obliged to heed its contents if relevant to the complaint.

Quota and registration

The quota scheme and registration under the Disabled Persons (Employment) Act 1944 cease to apply.

THE DETAILED REQUIREMENTS

The Disability Discrimination Act represents only a fraction of what the law entails for employers.

First, the Government has published Regulations to add to what is included in the Act itself. These include *The Disability Discrimination (Meaning of Disability) Regulations 1996* and the *Disability Discrimination (Employment) Regulations 1996* which deals largely with building regulations but also pay, occupational pension schemes, agricultural wages, and contract work. There is also *The Disability Discrimination Act (Questions and Replies) Order 1996* for use in connection with complaints, and the publication *Guidance on Matters to be Taken Into Account in Determining Questions Relating to the Definition of Disability.*

Second, as mentioned earlier, the government has published a *Code of Practice for the Elimination of Discrimination in the Field of Employment Against Disabled Persons or People Who Have Had a Disability.*

Third, a body of case law is being built up and at the time of revising this book in early 2000, over 5,000 complaints had been made. Some examples of tribunal decisions and those of the Employment Appeal Tribunal, and, in one case, that of the Court of Appeal, are given in this chapter, as in some of the chapters in Part 1.

DISABILITY DEFINITION

Who is disabled?

Section 1 of Part I of the Act states that a person has a disability if he (*sic*) has a physical or mental impairment which has a 'substantial and long-term adverse effect on his ability to carry out normal day-to-day activities'. Section 2 deals with past disabilities to include people who have had a disability, that is to say that it is now unlawful to discriminate against a person on the grounds of his or her past record of disability as with a person who currently has a disability. Physical impairment covers the senses, such as sight and hearing; mental impairment includes learning disabilities and mental illness.

Section I of the Act is supplemented by further details in Schedule 1 as to the meanings of certain expressions, for example that 'long term' is to be taken to mean 12 months.

ME is a Disability
(but the employer did not know)

O'Neill v Symm & Co Ltd

Ms O'Neill was employed as an accounts clerk from 3 September 1996 to 3 December 1996. In November, she was diagnosed as having myalgic encephalomyelitis (ME) and the following month was dismissed because she had taken 15-and-a-half days' sick leave since the beginning of her employment. A Reading industrial tribunal accepted that ME was a disability under the Act. It heard evidence to that effect from experienced medical practitioners.

It noted that ME is classified as a separate and recognisable disease of the central nervous system by the World Health Organisation and that in this case there was evidence that the applicant's condition had a 'long-term adverse effect'. It also noted that during her period of employment she was experiencing acute tiredness together with a number of other symptoms including reduced mobility, pains and cramps in her limbs, tender lymph glands, sore throat and persistent chest problems, all of which affected her ability to carry out normal day-to-day activities.

However, the tribunal rejected the claim for unlawful discrimination because it found that the 'employer' had not received the applicant's medical certificate and was 'unaware' that she had ME. Therefore the decision to dismiss was related to the absences but was not for a reason related to her disability. Similarly, although an adjustment to the applicant's working hours might have assisted in the management of the illness and could have been accommodated without too much difficulty, the 'employer could not reasonably have been expected to know that she had a disability'. Therefore, the duty to make adjustments did not apply.

11 June 1997; case no. 2700054/97. The Employment Appeal Tribunal upheld the decision on appeal.

In October 1998, the EAT gave detailed guidance in the correct approach to deciding whether a person has a disability within the meaning of the Act. This was in the case of *Goodwin v The Patent Office*. Mr Goodwin was dismissed from his job and complained to the tribunal. His application failed because the tribunal did not consider his impairment had a substantial adverse effect on his normal day-to-day activities. The EAT, however, allowed his appeal, Mr Justice Morrison urging tribunals to adopt an inquisitorial role and make explicit reference to the Code of Practice. The EAT gives the following guidance on the four limbs of the definition:

i) does the applicant have a physical or mental impairment? (If in doubt on a mental impairment, ascertain whether it is mentioned in the WHO ICD.)

ii) does that impairment affect the applicant's ability to carry out normal day-to-day activities, in *one* of the respects set out in the Act (Schedule 1)? (Carrying them out does not mean the ability to carry them out has not been impaired, eg a person may be able to cook but only with the greatest difficulty – this is important/significant – the focus required by the Act is on the things the applicant either cannot do or can only do with difficulty, rather than on the things the person can do.)

iii) is the adverse effect of the impairment substantial? EAT reminds that substantial means more than minor or trivial, rather than very large.

iv) is it long term, effectively twelve months?

The EAT also draws attention to the effect of medical treatment. This should be disregarded by tribunals who should deduce what the effects of the impairment would be without it.

The tribunals will wish to examine how the applicant's abilities had been affected at the material time, while *on* medication, then *without* the medical treatment the person has been receiving; what effects do they think there would have been but for the medication; the deduced effects?

Exclusions from the scope of the definition

Regulations made under Section 1 of the Act, *The Disability Discrimination (Meaning of Disability) Regulations 1996,* have the effect of excluding from the definition, as being treated as not amounting to an impairment for the purposes of the Act:

- addiction to alcohol, nicotine or any other substance (other than if medically caused);
- a tendency to set fires;

- a tendency to steal;
- a tendency to physical or sexual abuse of other persons;
- exhibitionism;
- voyeurism;
- seasonal allergic rhinitis (hay fever) (except if it aggravates the effect of another condition);
- a tattoo;
- body piercing for non-medical purposes.

Substantial effects

According to the published guidance document, a substantial effect is one which is more than minor or trivial, and which satisfies a general understanding of disability as a limitation going beyond the normal differences in ability between people. The time taken to carry out an activity by a person with an impairment should be taken into account, comparing it with a person who does *not* have the impairment; another factor is the way in which an activity is carried out in comparison with the way in which a person *without* the impairment might be expected to carry it out. The guidance in the Goodwin case (see above) is also helpful here.

Cumulative effects

An impairment (eg breathing difficulties) might not have a substantial adverse effect on normal day-to-day activities in any one category, but account should be taken of whether its effects on several categories taken together are substantial. It is also possible that a person may have more than one impairment, none of which is sufficient alone to have a substantial effect. In such a case, account should be taken of whether there is a substantial adverse effect overall on the person's ability to carry out normal day-to-day activities: for example, a minor impairment which affects physical coordination and an irreversible but minor injury to a leg, taken together, might have a substantial effect on ability. Again, a person with mild cerebral palsy might experience a number of minor effects such as fatigue, poor visual perception and difficult coordination and balance which, together, create substantial adverse effects on a range of normal day-to-day activities.

Effects of behaviour and of environment

Account should be taken of how far a person can reasonably be expected to manage the effects of an impairment to prevent or reduce its effects on normal day-to-day activities. If a person can behave in a particular way so that the impairment ceases to have a substantial effect, he or she would no longer meet the definition. If, however, such a coping strategy could cease to have that effect then this possibility should be taken into account. Also, to decide whether adverse effects are substantial may depend on, say, the temperature, time of day, or whether the person was tired or under stress. All such factors should be considered.

Effects of treatment

The Act provides that if an impairment is being treated or corrected, the impairment is to be treated as having the effect it would have *without* the measures in question. These measures include medical treatment or use of a prosthesis. This applies even if the measures result in the effects being completely under control or not at all apparent. An example given is that of a person who uses a hearing aid, where the question of whether his or her impairment has a substantial adverse effect is to be decided by reference to the hearing level without the aid. The exception to this is the use of spectacles or contact lenses to correct sight.

Progressive conditions

If a person has a progressive condition, eg multiple sclerosis, he or she will be treated as having an impairment which has a substantial adverse effect from the time it has *some* effect on their ability to carry out normal day-to-day activities.

Severe disfigurements

If an impairment consists of a severe disfigurement, it is to be treated as having a substantial effect on the person's ability to carry out normal day-to-day activities.

Normal day-to-day activities

An impairment is to be taken to affect the ability of the person concerned to carry out normal day-to-day activities *only* if it affects one of the following:

(a) mobility;
(b) manual dexterity;
(c) physical coordination;
(d) continence;
(e) ability to lift, carry or otherwise move everyday objects;
(f) speech, hearing or eyesight;
(g) memory or ability to concentrate, learn or understand; or
(h) perception of the risk of physical danger.

This list is exhaustive.

In deciding whether an effect on a day-to-day activity is a substantial adverse effect, account should be taken of factors such as the examples listed under each category of day-to-day activity below:

- **Mobility** This covers moving or changing position in a wide sense. Account should be taken of the extent to which a person can get around unaided or using an appropriate means of transport, can leave home with or without assistance, walk a short distance, climb stairs, travel in a car or on public transport, sit, stand, bend, reach or get around in an unfamiliar place.
- **Manual dexterity** This covers the ability to use hands and fingers with precision. Account should be taken of the extent to which a person can manipulate the fingers on each hand or coordinate the use of both hands together to do a task. This includes their ability to do things like pick up or manipulate small objects, communicate through writing or typing or operate a range of equipment manually. Loss of function in the dominant hand would be expected to have a greater effect than equivalent loss in the non-dominant hand.
- **Physical coordination** This covers balanced and effective interaction of body movement, including hand and eye coordination. In the case of a child, it is necessary to take account of the level of achievement which would be normal for a person of that particular age. In all cases, account should be taken of the ability to carry out activities such as walking and using the hands at the same time.
- **Continence** This covers the ability to control urination and/or defecation. Account should be taken of the frequency and extent of the loss of control and the age of the individual.
- **Ability to lift, carry or otherwise move everyday objects** Account should be taken of a person's ability to repeat these functions or, for example, to bear weights over a reasonable period of time. Everyday objects might include such items as books, a kettle of water, bags of shopping, a briefcase, an overnight bag, a chair or other piece of light furniture.
- **Speech, hearing or eyesight** This covers normal day-to-day activities which involve the ability to speak, hear or see and includes face-to-face, telephone and written communication.
  - **Speech** Account should be taken of how far a person is able to speak clearly at a normal pace and rhythm and to understand someone speaking normally in his or her native language. It is necessary to consider any effects that affect speech patterns or impede the acquisition or processing of one's native language, for example the problems experienced by someone who has had a stroke.

- **Hearing** If a person uses a hearing aid or similar device, it is necessary to consider the effect experienced if the person is not using the hearing aid or device. The level of background noise should be within such a range and of such a type that most people would be able to hear adequately.
- **Eyesight** If a person's sight is corrected by spectacles or contact lenses, or could be corrected by them, what needs to be considered is the effect remaining while they are wearing spectacles or lenses, in light of a level and type normally acceptable to most people for day-to-day activities.

• **Memory and the ability to concentrate, learn or understand** Account should be taken of the person's ability to remember, organize his or her thoughts, plan a course of action and execute it, or take in new knowledge. This includes considering whether the person learns to do things more slowly than is normal. Account should be taken of whether the person has persistent and significant difficulties in reading text written in standard English or straightforward numbers.

• **Perception of the risk of physical danger** This includes both the under- and overestimation of physical danger, including danger to one's well-being. Account should be taken, for example, of whether a person is inclined to neglect basic functions such as eating, drinking, sleeping, keeping warm and personal hygiene. Also, reckless behaviour which puts the person at risk or excessive avoidance behaviour without a good cause must be observed.

The authors are indebted to the published guidance on these matters and the examples given in it of how the above categories might be applied in particular circumstances. See *Guidance on Matters to be Taken Into Account in Determining Questions Relating to the Definition of Disability* (The Stationery Office, £7.50).

Long-term effects

For the purposes of deciding whether a person is disabled, long term is to be taken as 12 months, that is, has lasted 12 months, is likely to last 12 months or for the rest of the person's life. It is not necessary for the *effect* to be the same throughout the relevant period, only that the impairment continues to have or be likely to have an effect on the ability to carry out normal day-to-day activities.

Recurring effects

If an impairment has had, but then ceases to have, a substantial adverse effect on a person's ability to carry out normal day-to-day activities, the substantial effect is to be treated as continuing if it is likely to recur.

DISCRIMINATION BY EMPLOYERS

Section 4 of the Act sets out the kinds of situation in which it is unlawful for an employer to discriminate against a disabled person for a reason that relates to the person's disability, and which cannot be shown to be justified. These are:

In recruitment

- the arrangements made for the purpose of determining to whom should be offered employment;
- the terms of employment offered;
- a deliberate refusal to offer employment.

Murphy v *Sheffield Hallam University*

Mr Murphy, who is profoundly deaf, had stated this on his application form, but no interpreter was provided at interview. The complaint that this was unlawful disability discrimination was upheld by the tribunal and Mr Murphy was awarded £2,500 for injury to feelings.

11 November 1998, case no. 2800489/98

In employment

- the terms of employment afforded;
- the opportunities for promotion, transfer, training or any other benefit;
- a deliberate refusal to afford such opportunities;
- dismissal or subjecting the disabled employee to any other detriment.

This last item could provide for any form of discrimination not covered by the earlier categories to be caught in the net, though as yet there is no view on what 'any other detriment' might include. Some kind of harassment on account of disability has been suggested.

However, what is *not* covered is the provision of benefits (which includes facilities and services) to the disabled employee if the employer is concerned with the provision of the same benefits to the public *unless*, that is, the provision differs in a material respect from the provision of the benefits by the employer to the employees, *or* is regulated by his contract of employment *or* the benefits relate to training. A useful example and a legal opinion on this rather complex part of the Act are given in *Disability Discrimination: Law and practice* (Doyle, 1996):

For example, the employer might be a bank providing loans to the public and loans to its employees (perhaps at favourable rates of interest). The exceptions are designed to prevent unnecessary overlap with the provisions in Part III of the Act outlawing discrimination in the provision of goods, facilities and services. The intention is that if an employer offers goods, facilities or services to its employees in the same way as it offers them to members of the public, but disabled employees receive discriminatory treatment in that provision, then their right of action falls under Part III of the Act if at all. Nevertheless, Part II of the Act will continue to apply to such discriminatory treatment if the provision of goods, facilities and services to the employer's employees is not identical to such provision to the public or is an incident of the employment contract or relates to training.

Meaning of discrimination

Section 5 deals with the meaning of discrimination which, put simply, is that if an employer treats a disabled person less favourably than he would another individual for some reason that relates to the disability, then that is discrimination, *provided* the employer cannot show that the treatment is justified. The employer also discriminates if he or she fails to comply with the duty of 'reasonable adjustment' as in Section 6 (dealt with in the following section) so long as he or she cannot show that that failure to comply is justified. (Interestingly, it is not unlawful to discriminate in *favour* of a disabled person!)

DISMISSAL – AND LINKS WITH EARLIER LEGISLATION

In cases of disabled people being unfairly dismissed from their jobs it is open to them to claim that their employer has acted unlawfully, ie has discriminated against them. Under pre-existing legislation for employment protection, it was possible to claim that they had been unfairly dismissed. An employer had to be able to demonstrate that the dismissal had been both fair and reasonable. While reasonableness in a case turned on its own facts and there were no absolute principles, fairness had to be due to one of the following:

1. capability – ill health/skill;
2. conduct, eg absenteeism;
3. redundancy;
4. contravention of the law; or
5. some other reason, eg incompatibility.

It is likely that item 1 above will be a natural heading in many cases of dismissal of disabled people and regard might well be given to its precedents in dealing with cases under the DDA. For the claimant, there would be a strong temptation to proceed under the DDA since the compensation available has no limit, whereas under the unfair dismissal route, any compensation is subject to a ceiling. Also, there is a qualifying period of service under unfair dismissal but no such similar requirement under the DDA.

Indeed, dismissal is proving to be the major source of complaints made under the Act, consistently representing over half the complaints made. As mentioned in Part 1 of the book and above, claims of unfair dismissal may be linked with complaints under the DDA enabling tribunals to order reinstatement under unfair dismissal legislation, and uncapped compensation (see, for example, *Kirker* v *British Sugar plc* in which a visually-impaired chemist was awarded compensation of £103,000, later raised to £167,000 when it was ruled that the awards were taxable).

Paul Brown, Barrister, has drawn our attention to earlier helpful decisions.

Seymour v *British Airways Board*, 1983

The EAT held that a person who was both registered and disabled was entitled to special consideration by his employer, which included looking at his personal circumstances before deciding to dismiss him. In that case, the employer had done so and the decision to dismiss was reasonable.

However, the comments in the Seymour case were that where the employee was known to be disabled when he was employed, it would be particularly difficult for an employer to justify dismissing that employee for incapability, and in these circumstances, the employer may be expected to absorb the predictable consequences of the disability or illness, eg absence (as occurred in the case *Kerr* v *Atkinson Vehicles (Scotland) Ltd* in 1974).

Paul Brown also records the difference in approach between the DDA and the earlier situation. Whereas S 98 ERA 1996 suggests that dismissal for capability is potentially fair, subject to the duty of reasonableness, the DDA states that dismissal for disability is discrimination, subject to the defence of justification. Further, while S 98(4) ERA is neutral as to where the burden of proving reasonableness lies, the DDA expressly places the burden of proving justification (see below) on the employer.

People Management (16 April 1998, pp 23, 24) carried a substantial article on dismissal on health grounds by Gill Sage of Simpson Millar, and with her kind permission, it is reproduced here.

Health Warning

Firms that dismiss staff on health grounds should take care not to fall foul of the Disability Discrimination Act.

Employers with twenty (NB now fifteen) or more staff – the threshold of the Disability Discrimination Act (DDA) – can no longer rely on ill-health as a fair reason for dismissal.

They must consider whether an employee has a disability and where reasonable adjustments could be made in order to keep them in the workplace. It is also clear that the law of frustration (treating an employment contract as having ended when an employee is incapable of any performance under the contract) will no longer operate when an employee is temporarily incapable of performing his or her duties as the result of a long-term medical condition.

Some useful guidance on interpretation of the Act was given recently in *Cox* v *The Post Office* (IT/1301162/97) in which a dismissal that had been handled under a union-agreed attendance procedure was successfully challenged. Cox had been employed by the Post Office since 1984 and had disclosed his asthmatic condition on joining. His absence record caused him to receive various informal warnings under an attendance procedure that defined basic standards of attendance and 'trigger points' at which employees would receive warnings and, ultimately, face dismissal.

Cox received his first formal warning in 1993, because he had taken 23 days off over the year, 17 of which were caused by his asthma. He also received a formal warning in 1994 after taking time off with 'flu. In the same year, he took three days off for a migraine and then a further nine days with an asthma-related respiratory infection.

He was formally interviewed about his absence record in November 1994, but was not dismissed. He took seven further days off sick over the next six months and was interviewed again in May 1995. In December that year he took 16 days' sick leave for asthma and a four-day absence in January 1996 with a viral infection, again asthma related. At this stage, the employee was dismissed, but the action was overturned through an internal appeals procedure.

In August 1996 Cox attended work, but collapsed and was taken to hospital. He was diagnosed as having exhaustion, but it was unclear whether the condition was brought on by his asthma. One of the reasons for the collapse was that the weather was exceptionally hot that week and the ventilation in the office was poor (the windows could not be opened). This fact was raised during the appeals procedure, but the employer gave no evidence to show that it had checked if the windows would open or whether this had contributed to Cox's collapse. He was dismissed at last in March 1997 on the grounds of his unsatisfactory attendance.

The tribunal established the following principles from this case:

- asthma is a physical impairment that has an adverse effect on the employee's ability to carry out normal day-to-day activities and is, therefore, a disability;
- to apply an attendance procedure to disability-related absences is discriminatory;
- dismissal over disability-related absences is discriminatory and unfair.

The employer should have discounted all of the disability-related absences before applying the attendance procedure.

To avoid breaching the DDA, it is essential to seek medical advice on the nature of the illness, its long-term prognosis and whether any adjustments could be made to the workplace to allow an early return to work. It is then essential to consult the employee and any representatives to discuss the condition in the light of the medical evidence. The employer should also consider any representations made by the employee.

No decision to terminate an employee's contract on the grounds of ill-health or to subject someone to any other detriment should now be taken solely on the basis of absence from the workplace. Even if the diagnosis of the illness is unclear, any substantial, long-term medical problem that has an adverse effect on normal day-to-day activities may amount to a disability under the DDA. This was clearly illustrated in *Howden* v *Capital Copiers (Edinburgh) Ltd* in which an employee having abdominal pain took 35 and a half days' sick leave and was dismissed, but was later awarded £12,659 in compensation by the tribunal.

A hasty dismissal may outweigh the cost of following a fair procedure that allows for full consideration of an employee's ill health based on consultation, a full medical opinion and mutually agreed strategies. If the employee then refuses to co-operate with a fair procedure by, for example, refusing to change working practices in line with occupational health service advice, then any dismissal may not be automatically unfair.

In order to avoid unfair dismissal and disability discrimination claims, cases of ill-health must be handled carefully. Employers with twenty (now fifteen) or more employees should conduct an audit of all staff to see if they have any long-term health problems that may be considered disabilities under the DDA, and which should be taken into account when managing sickness absence.

Another significant feature of the dismissal aspect of the legislation is the failure to make reasonable adjustments, and this is dealt with more fully below, under that heading.

Justification

If the employer does rely upon the defence of justification, subsection 5(3) makes clear that treatment is justified if, but *only* if, the reason for it is both material to the circumstances of the particular case and substantial. Professor Doyle again:

> An employer will always be able to defend a discrimination complaint by proving that the alleged discriminatory act was not for a reason which relates to the disabled complainant's disability ... The justification defence in subsection 5 (3) clearly only applies where an employer *has* treated a disabled person less favourably for a disability-related reason. In other words, the Act envisages that there will be cases where, despite the merit principle, an employer could take lawful account of a person's disability.

The inference from all this seems to be that if a person is denied employment or conditions of employment that he or she would have expected had they not been disabled, or reasonable adjustments (see below) had not been made, discrimination could be thought to have occurred. The procedure for making a complaint is explained later in the chapter. However, it could be argued that if the guidelines on fair treatment in Part 1 of this book are followed, these issues would be avoided or dealt with more easily.

MAKING REASONABLE CHANGES – DUTY OF AN EMPLOYER TO MAKE ADJUSTMENTS

Section 6 of the Act is a particularly complex section. It requires in effect that if any arrangements made by an employer, or if any physical feature of premises occupied by an employer, place the disabled person at a substantial disadvantage in comparison with non-disabled people, the employer has a *duty* to take reasonable steps to overcome that disadvantage. This applies at all stages of employment including recruitment, terms of employment, promotion, training, transfer or any other benefit. Helpfully, the Act gives examples of the type of steps that an employer might have to take to comply with this duty – the 'duty of reasonable adjustment':

(a) making adjustments to premises;
(b) allocating some of the disabled person's duties to another person:
(c) transferring him to fill an existing vacancy;
(d) altering his working hours;
(e) assigning him to a different place of work;

(f) allowing him to be absent during working hours for rehabilitation, assessment or treatment;

(g) giving him or arranging for him to be given, training;

(h) acquiring or modifying equipment;

(i) modifying instructions or reference manuals;

(j) modifying procedures for testing or assessment;

(k) providing a reader or interpreter;

(l) providing supervision.

(This list is not exhaustive.)

However, subsection (4) of Section 6 states:

In determining whether it is reasonable for an employer to have to take a particular step in order to comply with subsection (1) (ie reasonable steps), regard shall be had in particular, to:

(a) the extent to which taking the step would prevent the effect in question;

(b) the extent to which it is practicable for the employer to take the step;

(c) the financial and other costs which would be incurred by the employer in taking the step and the extent to which taking it would disrupt any of his activities;

(d) the extent of the employer's financial and other resources;

(e) the availability to the employer of financial or other assistance with respect to taking the step.

The duty to make reasonable adjustments is, therefore, not absolute and applies only where the disabled person is at a substantial disadvantage, and the steps taken must be reasonable in all the circumstances.

The word 'reasonable' has been criticized for being too imprecise. However, to be absolutely precise in circumstances involving a wide range of disabilities, would be impossible. Therefore, leaving it to the judgment of independent tribunals to settle individual interpretations of reasonableness is as good a way as any of securing a fair outcome of complaints. The *Code of Practice for the Elimination of Discrimination in the Field of Employment Against Disabled Persons or Persons Who Have Had a Disability* (The Stationery Office, £9.95) gives further guidance and a number of useful examples of what might or might not be regarded as reasonable. These include giving extra time to an applicant to carry out a letter writing test which, because it would not inconvenience the employer very much, would be a reasonable adjustment; while an employer would be unlikely to be required to widen a particular doorway for a wheelchair user if there were an easy alternative route to the same destination.

Other helpful general guidance on costs includes the suggestion that it would be reasonable for an employer to spend at least as much on making an adjustment to enable a disabled employee to keep his or her job as might be spent on recruiting and retraining a replacement. Other factors that need to be taken into account include the resources invested in an employee, the employee's length of service and level of skill and knowledge, quality of relationships with clients and level of pay.

Kenny v Hampshire Constabulary

Mr Kenny, an IT graduate, was offered a post as a programmer subject to arrangements being made for his need of assistance when going to the toilet. The employer thought other workers would volunteer. They didn't. A support worker was requested through Access to Work but before a decision was made, the job offer was withdrawn. The tribunal dismissed the complaint and EAT upheld the decision: 'It was going too far to expect employers to take account of employees' care needs', but allowed the appeal that the tribunal had failed to consider whether the employer was justified in not waiting for the support worker.

EAT, 14 October 1998

Guidance on the procedure for tribunals to go through is given in *Morse v Wiltshire County Council* (see page 138).

Arrangements made by or on behalf of an employee

The Act appears to make a distinction between its application to recruitment, conditions of service, promotion, transfer, training or any other benefit on the one hand, and to dismissal on the other. Some lawyers have therefore taken the view that an employer is not obliged to make reasonable adjustment to any arrangements, eg in the hours of work, in considering whether to retain or dismiss a disabled person. As a result, in relation to dismissal, it is only the duty regarding physical features (see below) which applies. Other lawyers consider that if this is what is intended, then it is difficult to reconcile it with some of the specific examples given in the Act, eg allocating some of the disabled person's duties to another person.

There is no obvious reason why an employer should be obliged to consider such matters when determining, say, promotion, when he or she is not obliged to do so when deciding to dismiss an employee. While that appears to be the consequence of the Act as it is drafted, some lawyers feel that this interpretation is so absurd it cannot be what was originally intended. However, at least one tribunal has taken the wording as it is presently drafted: *Clark* v *Novacold* (Hull, 21 August 1997) held that the duty to make reasonable adjustments does *not* apply to dismissal. The EAT then found that the tribunal had erred in taking that view. However, when the case went to the Court of Appeal (the first to go that far), the Court held that the duty does not apply to dismissal, though the dismissed employee *may* bring a case for pre-dismissal discrimination.

Comparators

The major issue in *Clark* v *Novacold*, however, was that of the correct comparator to be used to determine whether a disabled person has been treated less favourably for a reason which related to their disability than others to whom that reason did not apply. Guidance was given in the Court of Appeal (Mummery L J): '. . . in the case of an employee absent from work for a disability-related reason, the correct comparison is with the treatment of employees who are not absent, rather than with an employee absent for the same time for a reason unrelated to the disability. If the employee has suffered less favourable treatment, then the focus is on justification and reasonable adjustment.'

Redundancy selection

Note that the duty applies also to selection for redundancy, and offers of alternative employment:

Hardy v *Gower Furniture Ltd*

A disabled forklift driver scored lowest on a redundancy selection because of his disabilities. He was offered alternative employment which he could not do and was made redundant when he rejected the offer. Held: unlawful discrimination. If Mr Hardy had not been disabled, he would not have been selected for redundancy.

20 July 1997, case no. 18002093/97

On the other hand:

Morse v Wiltshire County Council

In this case Mr Morse, a roadworker, was selected for redundancy because he could not drive. His claim was dismissed but the EAT said that a tribunal must go through a number of steps sequentially in dealing with allegations of failure to consider the duty to make a reasonable adjustment:

1. decide whether there is a duty to the employer in the particular case, ie a substantial disadvantage;
2. if so, decide whether the employer has taken such steps as it is reasonable in all the circumstances, ie to prevent the substantial disadvantage in comparison with non-disabled people;
3. if so, enquiring whether the employer could reasonably have taken any of the steps set out in the Act (these are only examples).

If the tribunal (having followed the above) finds that the employer has failed to comply with the duty, it must decide whether the employer's failure is justified.

Physical features of premises

The duty of reasonable adjustment applies to physical features of premises occupied by the employer. 'Physical feature' is not defined in the Act but Section 6 (8) enables regulations to deal with issues of definition. The Government has made clear in the regulations that the term 'physical feature of premises' includes any of the following, whether temporary or permanent:

- any feature arising from the design or construction of a building on the premises;
- any feature on the premises or any approach to, exit from or access to such a building;
- any fixtures, fittings, furnishings, furniture, equipment or materials, in or on the premises;
- any other physical element or quality of any land comprised in the premises.

(Taken from *The Disability Discrimination (Employment) Regulations 1996*.)

Pay and occupational pensions

The Disability Discrimination (Employment) Regulations 1996 also state:

Pay

3 (1) For the purposes of Section 5 of the Act treatment is to be taken to be justified if it results from applying to the disabled person a term or practice:

(a) under which the amount of a person's pay is wholly or partly dependent on that person's performance; and
(b) which is applied to all of the employer's employees or to all of a class of his employees which includes the disabled person but which is not defined by reference to any disability.

(2) Arrangements consisting of the application to a disabled person of a term or practice of the kind referred to in paragraph (1) above are not to be taken to place that disabled person at a substantial disadvantage of the kind mentioned in section 6(1) of the Act.

(3) Nothing in this regulation affects the operation of section 6 of the Act in relation to any arrangements or physical features of premises which, by placing a disabled person at a substantial disadvantage, cause reduced performance by him.

Occupational pension schemes

4 (1) For the purposes of section 5(1) of the Act, less favourable treatment of a disabled person is to be taken to be justified in the circumstances described in paragraph (2) below if it results from applying the eligibility conditions set for receiving any benefit referred to in paragraph (3) below or from determining the amount of any such benefit.

(2) The circumstances are that by reason of the disabled person's disability (including any clinical prognosis flowing from the disability) the cost of providing any benefit referred to in paragraph (3) below is likely to be substantially greater than it would be for a comparable person without that disability.

(3) The benefits are those provided under an occupational pension scheme in respect of any of the following:

(a) termination of service;
(b) retirement, old age or death; or
(c) accident, injury, sickness or invalidity.

Uniform rates of contributions

5 For the purposes of section 5 of the Act, treatment is always to be taken to be justified if an employer requires from a disabled person the same rate of contribution to an occupational pension scheme as he requires from his other employees (or from any class of his employees which includes the disabled person but which is not defined

by reference to any disability), notwithstanding that the disabled person is not eligible under that scheme, for a reason related to his disability, to receive a benefit or to receive a benefit at the same rate as a comparable person to whom that reason does not apply.

Contract workers

The position of contract workers, including those placed by an agency, is dealt with in the Act. Generally speaking, the Act and Regulations apply to the hiring employers as if they were the actual employer of the contract worker, that is, if that employer has 15 or more employees. Therefore, the same definition of discrimination, including the need to justify less-favourable treatment and the duty to make reasonable adjustment, applies as to any other employer. Of course, in considering what might be regarded as reasonable in these cases, it is appropriate to take account of the length of time the contract worker(s) will be with the hiring employer, ie it might well be unreasonable for the employer to have to make certain adjustments if they will be engaged for only a short time. The Act also applies to an employment business (agency) which has 15 or more employees, including people hired out to others. However, the Act (Section 12) does specifically make it unlawful for a principal, ie the hirer, to discriminate against a disabled person in relation to contract work:

(a) in the terms on which he allows him to do that work;
(b) by not allowing him to do it or continue to do it;
(c) in the way he affords him access to any benefits or by refusing or deliberately omitting to afford him access to them; or
(d) by subjecting him to any other detriment.

If you use contract workers, you are advised specifically to study the Code of Practice on this matter and consider your legal position very carefully.

Provisions applying to trade unions

The Act says that it is unlawful for a trade organization to discriminate against a disabled person:

(a) in the terms on which it is prepared to admit the person to membership; or
(b) by refusing to accept, or deliberately not accepting, an application for membership.

It is also unlawful to discriminate against a disabled *member*:

140

(a) in the way it affords him access to any benefits or by refusing or deliberately omitting to afford him access to them;

(b) by depriving him of membership, or varying the terms on which he is a member; or

(c) by subjecting him to any other detriment.

Note, however, that while the Act defines discrimination by a trade organization in similar terms to those relating to an employer, and therefore, the need to justify less-favourable treatment obtains, the duty to make reasonable adjustments (Section 15) was not to be brought into force until a later date. This was the only part of the employment provisions not implemented in December 1996 – the duty to make reasonable adjustments came into force on 1 October 1999, though the duty to make reasonable adjustments 'as a result of physical features of premises' will not be introduced until 2004. The Government has now published a further Code of Practice on this aspect of the Act: *Code of Practice – Duties of Trade Organisations to Their Disabled Members and Applicants* (The Stationery Office, £9.95).

COMPLAINTS

Disabled people who feel that an employer has unfairly discriminated against them may complain to an employment tribunal. Both the complainant and the respondent (employer) may request a conciliation officer to try to promote a settlement of the complaint. Conciliation officers might also try to promote a settlement if they consider they have a reasonable chance of success. Thus, the grievance can be settled without a tribunal hearing. The time limit for a complaint is three months from the time of the deed complained of, though the tribunal may consider an out-of-time complaint if it considers it just and equitable to do so.

If a complaint is upheld by a tribunal, it may order the respondent to take action to obviate or reduce the cause of the complaint, to pay compensation or to make a declaration as to the rights of the complainant and the respondent in relation to the matter complained about. If you wish to know more about tribunal procedures, various leaflets may be obtained from the Employment Tribunals Service at 19–29 Woburn Place, London WC1H 0LU. You should note, however, that further powers of enforcement are contained in the Disability Rights Commission Act 1999, which is dealt with at the end of the next chapter and reproduced as Appendix 2.

The Act does not require employers to resolve disputes, but they might try to do so, looking to their grievance procedures when necessary to prevent matters reaching the formal complaint stage.

QUESTIONNAIRE PROCEDURE

The government has made an order, The Disability Discrimination (Questions and Replies) Order 1996, closely following the existing secondary legislation made under the Sex Discrimination and Race Relations Acts. It mirrors those Acts by prescribing the form of questionnaire to be served on a respondent within three months, but differs from those Acts in that additional questions and statements need to be included in the scheduled forms to cover the duty of reasonable adjustment (see above) imposed by the Disability Discrimination Act, but not found in other anti-discrimination legislation. The order also prescribes a form for the respondent's reply. It is helpful to set out the two prescribed forms, which are as follows:

SCHEDULE 1
THE DISABILITY DISCRIMINATION ACT 1995 s56 (2)(a).
QUESTIONNAIRE OF COMPLAINANT

To .... *(name of person to be questioned*

.... *(the respondent))*

of .... *(address)*

1 I, ... *(name of complainant)*

   of .... *(address)*

consider that you may have discriminated against me contrary to the Disability Discrimination Act 1995 ('the Act') by unjustifiably

(a) for a reason relating to my disability, treating me less favourably than you treat or would treat people to whom that reason does not or would not apply, or

(b) failing to take steps which it was reasonable in all the circumstances to have to take to prevent your employment arrangements or premises putting me at a substantial disadvantage compared with people who are not disabled.

---

2 *(Give details including a factual description of the treatment received or the failure complained of. Describe any relevant circumstances leading up to this and include any relevant dates or approximate dates.)*

3 I consider this treatment or failure on your part may have been unlawful [because ....] (complete if you wish to give reasons, otherwise delete).

4 Do you agree that the statement in paragraph 2 above is an accurate description of what happened? If not, in what respect do you disagree or what is your version of what happened?

5 Do you accept that your treatment of me or any failure complained of was unlawful? If not-

(a) why not,
(b) do you consider your treatment of me or your failure to take action was justified for any material or substantial reason(s)?

6 *(Any other questions you wish to ask.)*

7 My address for any reply you may wish to give to the questions raised above is [that set out in paragraph I above] [the following address]

.... (signature of complainant)

.... (date)

NB By virtue of section 56(3) of the Act, this questionnaire and any reply are (subject to the provisions of section 56 and any orders made under that section) admissible in proceedings under Part II of the Act and a tribunal may draw any inference it considers is just and equitable from a failure without reasonable excuse to reply within a reasonable period, or from an evasive or equivocal reply, including any inference that the respondent has discriminated unlawfully under Part II of the Act.

SCHEDULE 2
THE DISABILITY DISCRIMINATION ACT 1995 s56 (2)(b).
REPLY BY THE RESPONDENT

To   .... *(name of complainant)*

of   .... *(address)*

1   I, ... *(name of respondent)*

    of .... *(address)*

hereby acknowledge receipt of the questionnaire signed by you and dated

.... which was served on me on .... *(date)*.

2   *I agree that the statement in paragraph 2 of the questionnaire is an accurate description of what happened.

*I disagree with the statement in paragraph 2 of the questionnaire in that:

....

....

3   I accept/dispute that my treatment of you or any failure to take action on my part was unlawful.

*My reasons for disputing this are ....

....

*I consider my treatment of you or my failure to take action was justified for the following material and substantial reason(s).

(Include any reasons which in your view explain or justify your treatment of the applicant or any decision not to take action.)

4   *(Replies to questions in paragraph 6 of the questionnaire.)*

*5 I have deleted (in whole or in part) the paragraphs numbered .... above, since I am unable/unwilling to reply to the relevant questions in the correspondingly numbered paragraphs(s) of the questionnaire for the following reasons:

....

....

.... Signature of respondent

.... Date

*delete as appropriate

.... *Henley* 5th November 1996

Minister of State Department for Education and Employment

It is open to the complainants to include at item 6 of Schedule 1 any other questions they wish to ask. These might be taken from the following examples:

The advertisement and the job description

Please provide a job description for the above post.

Please provide a person specification for the above post.

Please provide details of the terms and conditions of employment for the above post.

When, where and by what method was the above post advertised?

Please provide a copy of the advertisement(s) for the above post stating when and where it appeared.

The recruitment procedure

Please describe your normal recruitment procedure.

Please describe the recruitment procedure for the above post.

If the recruitment procedure for the above post differed from the usual procedure please describe how and why.

Shortlisting

How many of the applicants for the above post were:

(a) non-disabled
(b) disabled?

Please describe the criteria used to shortlist for interview.

Please state the names and job titles of those people involved in the shortlisting process.

Please state the date on which the shortlist was drawn up.

How many of the individuals shortlisted were:

(a) non-disabled
(b) disabled?

Please explain why I was not shortlisted.

The interviews

Please state the date on which the interviews took place.

How many of those interviewed were:

(a) non-disabled
(b) disabled?

Please state the sex, marital status, age, number and ages of children, qualifications, experience and disabilities of each candidate interviewed.

Please state the sex, marital status, age, number and ages of children, qualifications, experience and disabilities of successful candidate/s.

Please explain why the successful candidate/s was/were appointed.

Please state the date on which the successful candidate/s was/were appointed.

Please explain why each of the unsuccessful candidates was not appointed.

Please explain why I was not appointed.

Please state the names and job titles of the interviewers.

Is there a list of the questions asked of all the candidates? If so, please provide a copy; if not, please state why there is not such a list.

Please provide a copy of any interview notes made in respect of each of the candidates.

Questions at interview

Please state the nature of disability of each applicant for the above post.

Please state which of the above candidate/s was/were interviewed.

Please state which of the above candidate/s was/were appointed to the post.

Please explain why each of the above candidate/s was/were not selected for the interview.

Why was I asked

(1) ....

(2) ....

(3) ....

[The question(s) considered to have been discriminatory.]

Were non-disabled candidates asked these questions?

Were all disabled candidates asked these questions?

Provision of equal opportunities

Please provide a list of your staff showing the job title, sex, length of service and disability of all job-holders.

Please provide a list of the [title of the job applied for] employed by you showing their sex, marital status, length of service and disability.

Are you aware of the *Code of Practice*; if so, do you have a copy of the *Code?*

What steps have you taken to implement the *Code of Practice?*

What training have staff involved in recruitment and selection received relating to the *Code of Practice?*

Please provide a copy of your Equal Opportunities Policy.

(With acknowledgement to Ruth Harvey, Partner, Sheridans, Solicitors – Source: EOC and CRE)

VICTIMIZATION

The Act makes it unlawful to victimize people who make use of or try to make use of their rights under the Act. People who help disabled people are also protected from being victimized.

LIKELY IMPACT OF THE DDA

While it is too early to say just how big an impact the legislation will have on employment and human resources practices in the UK, there is no doubt that managers need to prime themselves on the likely implications. This chapter has tried to highlight the main issues in a general way, but readers should consult their lawyers about any specific legal challenges with which they are faced. The context of this book is broader than the legal requirements, though the authors feel that if the messages in the book are followed as regards good practices in employing disabled people – or for that matter any people – on an equal opportunity basis, then there will be a good chance of the spirit of the legislation being more than satisfied. As stated earlier, over 5,000 complaints have been made at the time of revision, over half of them for dismissal. Many were settled without reaching tribunals. The most publicized was also the most instructive:

Failure to Make Reasonable Adjustment

Tarling v *Wisdom Toothbrushes Ltd*

Mrs Tarling, who was born with a club foot, had worked for Wisdom Toothbrushes for almost 18 years. By 1996, her condition was causing her pain and discomfort, limiting her ability to carry out normal day-to-day activities. The company sought and received expert advice that she might be better able to perform her duties using a 'Grahl' chair, costing around £1,000. Instead of acting on the advice, the company provided the employee with a series of 'ordinary' chairs.

Throughout this time, she was not achieving her production targets and the company began disciplinary proceedings which resulted in her dismissal. She claimed unlawful disability discrimination. A Bury St Edmunds industrial tribunal (Chair: D R Crome) was in no doubt that she had a disability and that she had been dismissed because of it.

Although the company had 'embarked on the perfectly proper and wholly laudable course of seeking advice', it failed to follow it through and make reasonable adjustments. It found that the employer could have taken the Grahl chair on free trial and that because of the assistance available, the

---

eventual cost to the employer might not have been more than £200. In the tribunal's view, this 'was not something that would have caused a significant problem and was a reasonable step within s.6(1) of the Act'. It awarded £1,200 for injury to feelings and, finding that the dismissal was unfair, ordered reinstatement on the basis that an appropriate accommodation be made.

24 June 1997; case no. 1500148/97.

A full report on the findings of a survey of early tribunal cases was published by the Institute for Employment Studies (Meager N et al, 1999).

8

Other areas covered by the Act

GOODS, FACILITIES, SERVICES AND PREMISES

This is a book about employment and takes account of the implications of the employment provisions of the DDA in some detail. It is not the appropriate place to dwell on the non-employment aspects. However, most employers will be running businesses which provide goods, facilities and/or services and, it should be noted, the exemption of employers of fewer than 15 employees does not apply to these provisions, only to them in their role as employers. *All* providers of goods, facilities and services and those selling, letting or managing premises are covered by the Act. It is unlawful for service providers, landlords or other persons to discriminate against disabled people in certain circumstances.

Among the services covered are those provided by hotels, banks, building societies, solicitors, local councils, advice agencies, pubs, theatres, shops, churches and the courts, and also public facilities like parks. On the property side, the Act covers all types, for example land, houses, flats, business premises, housing associations, hostels, estate and accommodation agencies and property developers. The only exceptions are: insurance; education (and for that see later in the chapter); transport vehicles (though the stations and airports are covered, and another part of the Act (Part V) allows the government to set access standards for buses, coaches, trains, trams and taxis); and any service not generally provided for members of the public, such as a private club that has strict selection procedures for regulating membership.

In all these cases, just as with the employment provisions, disabled people should not be treated less favourably because of their disability by those providing goods, facilities or services if the treatment cannot be justified.

> Discrimination occurs when a disabled person is treated less favourably than someone else and the treatment relates to the person's disability, it does not apply to another person, and cannot be justified.

From the first date of the Act's implementation, on 2 December 1996, subject to a few limited circumstances of justification, it has been unlawful to:

(1) refuse to provide, or deliberately not provide, a service to a disabled person when it is normally offered to other people;
(2) provide a lower standard of service, or in a worse manner;
(3) provide a service on less favourable terms.

From 1 October 1999 it has been unlawful for a service provider to fail to comply with the duty to make reasonable adjustments to policies, practices or procedures that make it impossible or unreasonably difficult for disabled people to use the service.

From 2004, it is intended that service providers will be required to make reasonable adjustments to the physical features of their premises to overcome physical barriers to access or provide the service by alternative means. We recommend you read *Code of Practice: Rights of access – goods, facilities, services and premises* (The Stationery Office £12.95).

EDUCATION

The position of education, from a manager's point of view, has to be considered under at least three distinct headings: Employment (Part II of the Act); Goods, facilities and services (Part III) and Education (Part IV), as well as the all-embracing Part I (Definition of disability) and the associated Regulations, Codes of Practice, and Guidance publications.

Education as an employer

All educational establishments and institutions which employ 15 or more people are subject to the employment provisions of the Act in just the same way as any other employer. The previous chapter on discrimination in employment and all the earlier relevant chapters apply equally to employers in this field.

Education as a provider of goods, facilities and services

Education which is funded or secured by a relevant body or provided at an establishment which is funded by such a body or by a Minister of the Crown, or any other establishment which is defined as a school, is excluded from these provisions. The Act defines a 'relevant body' as: a local education authority in England and Wales; an education authority in Scotland; the Funding Agency for Schools; the Further and Higher Education Funding Councils for England and Wales; the Scottish Higher Education Funding Council; the Teacher Training Agency; a voluntary body or a body of a prescribed kind. A school is as defined in the Further and Higher Education Act 1992 (Section 14 (5)) or the Education (Scotland) Act 1980 (Section 135 (1)).

The exclusion covers everyday educational activities, those which take place away from school or college premises, or out of normal hours, for example on field trips or visits.

Any incidental and ancillary services such as conference facilities or holiday accommodation offered on the same premises are, however, subject to the provisions on rights of access to goods, facilities and services as set out earlier in this chapter. In particular, student union facilities are covered by the Act just as if they were provided elsewhere; that is, they will be subject to the provisions of the Act in all respects.

Disability statements in education

However, the Act does require all schools, colleges of further education and higher education institutions to provide information about their provision for disabled students. This is done through the periodic publication of disability statements. Interested readers may obtain more information from Skill: National Bureau for Students with Disabilities (see Appendix 4).

Possible forthcoming changes in education

At the time of writing, the Government is consulting for and preparing a Bill to remove the exemptions of Education from Part III of the Act (Goods, facilities and services) in line with recommendations of the Disability Rights Task Force (see page 153).

TRANSPORT

Under Part V of the DDA, the Secretary of State can make regulations to ensure that disabled people can use public transport vehicles – taxis, buses, coaches, trains and trams. The regulations will ensure that disabled people can get on and off public transport vehicles safely, travel in them in safely and with reasonable comfort.

THE NATIONAL DISABILITY COUNCIL

Part VI of the DDA created the National Disability Council to advise the Government about disability issues and the implementation of the Act. However, this body has now been superseded by the Disability Rights Commission (see below).

DISABILITY RIGHTS COMMISSION ACT 1999

This is 'An act to establish a Disability Rights Commission and make provision as to its functions; and for the connected purposes' (27 July 1999). Unlike the DDA, this Act does not generally extend to Northern Ireland. See page 120 for a full list of the 15 commissioners appointed early in 2000 by the Secretary of State. The Commission's function started work on 25 April 2000. Its function goes well beyond that of the purely advisory role of the former National Disability Council (see above), and, like the Equal Opportunities Commission and Race Relations Commission, it is empowered to take up complaints on behalf of individual disabled people in certain cases: if the case raises a question of principle; if it is unreasonable to expect the applicant to deal with the case unaided (because of its complexity, because of the applicant's position in relation to another party, or for some other special reason); or if there is some other special consideration that makes it appropriate for the Commission to provide assistance. It may also be directed to carry out a formal investigation by the Secretary of State.

If it finds that anyone has committed or is currently committing an unlawful act, the Commission may prevent them from committing another or stop their current activity. Culprits may be required to produce an acceptable action plan with a view to seeking compliance, or to enter an agreement undertaking not to commit any further unlawful acts of the same kind or, if appropriate, to cease committing one. Failure to comply with such an undertaking entitles the Commission to apply to a county court or sheriff for an order. Full details are given in the statute which appears as Appendix 2. In addition, the Commission will give information and advice to businesses, employers, service providers and disabled people. It will produce new codes of practice and bring existing ones up to date, and conduct research and conciliation. More generally, the Commission has the following specific duties:

- to work towards the elimination of discrimination against disabled persons;
- to promote the equalization of opportunities for disabled people;
- to take such steps as it considers appropriate with a view to encouraging good practice in the treatment of disabled people (which, in employment matters, is what this book is about); and
- to keep under review the working of the Disability Discrimination Act 1995.

THE DISABILITY RIGHTS TASK FORCE

After the publication of the first edition of this book, a Disability Rights Task Force was set up on 3 December 1997 to look at the best ways of securing comprehensive enforceable rights for disabled people, and to make recommendations on the role and functions of a Disability Rights Commission. As we mentioned above, the Commission is now in place. The Task Force's recommendations on the functions of the Commission were published in December 1999. Some of its members have become commissioners on the Disability Rights Commission.

Its key recommendations were grouped into five categories:

- major extensions to the coverage of the DDA;
- public sector leadership in promoting equal opportunities;
- refinements to the detail of the DDA;
- use of non-legislative measures;
- further work.

Of the major extensions to the coverage of the DDA, the ending of exemption for education is the most significant and urgent. It has been regarded as astonishing that schools, colleges and universities are not acting unlawfully if they discriminate against students, but this is the case. The Government has been quick to act on this recommendation and has pledged to amend the Act in this respect, alongside other educational legislation, and the necessary Bill is now in preparation (see also page 151).

The DRT has emphasized the role that the public sector can play in promoting the equalization of opportunities for disabled people and has recommended that the barriers to the involvement of disabled people in public life should be removed. This latter point would be new to UK anti-discrimination legislation; they point to the need to review a specific statutory reference to physical disability as a reason for discharging a juror.

Regarding employment matters, the Task Force recommends that the provisions of the DDA should be broadened to include occupations currently excluded: the police, fire service, prison service and the armed forces. One particularly interesting recommendation relating this area is that the present defence of justification for failure to make a reasonable adjustment should be removed, and that the approach to reasonableness should be expanded to reflect valid justifications.

The DRT believes, however, that many changes in the lives of disabled people can be secured without recourse to legislation; for example, a voluntary-work code of good practice (but with a power to bring volunteers into coverage of civil rights legislation if necessary), guidance on access to shipping and air travel; manufacturing 'design for all'; more accessible products; and, in particular, the information accompanying them being in accessible formats.

More fundamentally, the Task Force has suggested that the definition of disability should be reviewed with a view to ensuring better coverage of mental-health conditions and the position of those with short-term, but severely disabling, conditions such as heart attacks, strokes or depression.

Postscript

Disability: some further issues

The new science of bioinformatics (the use of technology to organize gene knowledge) is bringing with it some fundamental questions. For example:

- Could a disabled child sue its parents for *not* using eugenics? It is already the case that mothers are held responsible for foetal alcohol syndrome.
- Might employers ask for a genetic readout before hiring someone? If so, this would disclose predispositions to particular diseases. However, predispositions are quite different from actually *having* the disease. How would the DDA deal with this?
- If such screening were made available but not used, what would the implications be for the workplace? Who would be liable, for example, in the case of an accident linked to an undetected disability?
- Who would pay for all the screening? People could sue for incomplete screening, for example if a test were available but not used and a disability subsequently arose.
- In cases of dismissal, will we hear 'gene type' used as a defence, eg 'I have a lazy gene', thus exonerating the person? Where will that leave employers?
- Does such a reductionist approach take away individual responsibility? In such a context, what place is there for empathy?
- In the context of an increasing insurance presence, how will insurance companies deal with all the above?
- How will managers deal with all of the above?

Appendix 1

List of common conditions

AIDS/HIV AIDS is short for Acquired Immune Deficiency Syndrome. It is caused by the human immunodeficiency virus or HIV. The virus can affect the body's normal defence against illness. Some people with HIV remain healthy for years without developing AIDS. People are recognized as having developed AIDS when the breakdown of the body's defences leads to serious infections and certain cancers. Between bouts of illness, even people with AIDS may be fit enough to work.

Arthritis is inflammation in joints and their surrounding structures. There are different kinds of arthritis, the most widely known being osteoarthritis (degenerative disorders of joints) and rheumatoid arthritis (the most common form of joint inflammation and damage). Pain management is an issue: there are various methods of treatment available.

Asthma gives people laboured, wheezy breathing, sometimes accompanied by coughing, due to an interference with the normal flow of air in the lungs. Asthma is usually caused by an allergy but can be precipitated by emotional factors or environmental changes. There are a number of ways of controlling asthma, although not everyone can be completely freed of the symptoms.

Autism can affect people of any age or ability. Recent research suggests that the main areas of life affected are relationships, the ability to empathize with others and social skills. Severe behavioural problems can be experienced by some people with autism.

Brittle bones is not a single condition but a group of several hundred disorders all caused by abnormalities in the production or structure of the protein component of bone known as collagen. Some brittle bone infants are born with fractures, and many people find they are faced with chronic pain and restriction of movement. Much can be done with orthopaedic surgery, although there is no complete cure.

Cancer may be present in many different ways but is relatively rare in young people. Young people tend to experience different forms of cancer from older people: eg leukaemia (affects white blood cells), lymphomas (cancer of the lymph nodes) or solid tumours (can occur anywhere in the body). The rate of progression and effectiveness of treatment varies from one cancer to another.

Cerebral palsy is a non-progressive disorder of movement and posture, caused by malfunction of, or damage to, the brain, usually occurring during pregnancy or at birth. Learning difficulties may or may not be present at the same time.

Coeliac syndrome is an inability of the body to tolerate or process gluten (present in cereal grains). The most common manifestations are stomach disorders, anaemia, irritable behaviour and poor growth rate. A change in diet can control the condition.

Colostomy: a colostomy operation is where the outlet for the bowel has to be diverted on to the abdomen, either temporarily or permanently, and a bag fixed to the skin to collect faeces. Someone who has just had this operation may take a little while to get used to his or her new routines, and may need extra rest. However, once the person has adapted, the effect on work should be minimal.

Cystic fibrosis is an hereditary disorder of the lungs and pancreas. There is no known cure but newly developed effective treatments (most notably of the lung infections and other illnesses caused by the malfunctioning of organs) mean that the life expectancy of people with this disease is increasing.

Diabetes means that the body is unable to produce the hormone insulin in the normal way. This results in the body being unable to control the utilization of sugar. With regular medication, which most people with diabetes are able to administer themselves, the condition need have little effect on their lives and consequently on their career prospects.

Down's Syndrome is a chromosomal disorder, where most affected people have an extra chromosome in each cell. The degree of learning difficulty varies from individual to individual. Some people with Down's Syndrome are more susceptible to respiratory infections or heart problems. As employees, people with Down's Syndrome can be very loyal and of pleasant disposition.

Dyslexia see Chapter 2 (page 28) on **specific learning difficulties**.

Epilepsy is the most common cause of recurrent fits. It is a symptom of a particular malfunctioning of part of the brain. Different kinds of epilepsy cause different kinds of fits. Some people experience an aura or warning and may have time to move from a potentially dangerous situation. Most people with epilepsy can control seizures by drugs, although some experience side-effects, for example drowsiness, which would have implications for the type of work suitable for them. Some people are photo-sensitive and seizures can be induced by bright or flickering lights; this can include a television or computer screen. Individuals will be able to tell you if this is the case. Even after experiencing a seizure, most people are able to resume work within the hour.

Haemophilia is an inherited condition, only affecting males, in which a person's blood does not clot properly. There are varying degrees of severity but advances in treatment mean that most people are able to treat themselves with intravenous injections when necessary and are able to carry out most activities. Some people with haemophilia may be physically disabled due to the number of 'bleeds' they have had, and the effect of the condition on their joints.

Heart disease usually begins in adulthood; although some people are born with heart disease and some children acquire it through diseases such as rheumatic fever. Surgery sometimes helps, but people with heart disease tend to remain frail. People who have heart **attacks** (myocardial infarction) generally need to avoid undue stress and heavy physical effort, but in most cases can continue otherwise to function normally.

HIV see **AIDS**.

ME (myalgic encephalomyelitis) is a physical illness characterized by exhaustion and overwhelming fatigue, muscle weakness, pain, mood changes and 'flu-like feelings. These symptoms tend to fluctuate from hour to hour and day to day, and are often made worse by physical and mental overactivity. Although the illness is not terminal, it can be extremely debilitating. At the moment there are no specific treatments, but many people feel better if they can get adequate rest and if they make certain changes to their lifestyle. Work capacity is obviously affected by the disease, although it is sometimes possible to alter routines so that the person can work within his or her limitations.

Multiple sclerosis is a progressive disease of the nervous system. The condition most commonly occurs after adolescence. It causes a variety of conditions: some degree of weakness and tremor is common. The illness cannot easily be cured but periods of remission are common and sometimes lengthy.

Muscular dystrophy is a progressive weakening of muscles whereby muscle cells are replaced by fat and fibrous tissue. People with some types of muscular dystrophy often have moderate learning difficulties. People with this condition have a short life-expectancy.

Psychoses are serious psychiatric conditions and can be permanent. People with psychoses may sometimes experience delusions, hallucinations, hyperactivity, withdrawn behaviour, depression, fragmented thinking and the inability to think and act rationally. It is possible to control this type of condition with medication, and for the person with psychosis to work successfully.

Rheumatism is not a diagnosis but a vague term which is used to describe aches and pains which seem to the person concerned to arise in the joints, muscles, ligaments or tendons, or in the connective tissues.

Rheumatoid arthritis: in young people, juvenile rheumatoid arthritis is the most common form. This condition is similar to arthritis in adults but the inflammation of the joints is from an unknown cause. The disease becomes inactive in some cases, but there is often serious joint deformity as a result of the arthritis. While the disease is active the person experiences intermittent stiffness, weakness and pain. All these symptoms can lead to stress.

RSI (repetitive strain injury) is caused by over-use of a particular joint, so that it becomes painful and possibly swollen. Once acquired, it can severely inhibit the person from carrying out similar kinds of work.

Schizophrenia (see also **psychoses**): it is incorrect to say that a diagnosis of schizophrenia implies a dual or split personality. People with schizophrenia can have difficulty in distinguishing between reality and delusion, and may sometimes appear withdrawn and lacking in social skills. Many people are able to manage their lives with the help of drugs, though these do have side-effects which are unpleasant, eg weight gain, restlessness. In some cases a complete recovery is possible.

Sickle cell anaemia is an inherited genetic disorder most prevalent in ethnic groups who originate from areas of the world where malaria is common. The disease causes painful blockages of blood vessels, anaemia and severe infection. There is no known treatment but symptoms can sometimes be treated and aggravating situations avoided.

Spina bifida is a weakness in the spinal canal caused during foetal development. People with spina bifida experience a range of physical disabilities affecting their trunk and lower limbs. Surgery can be successful in reducing some of the effects of this condition.

Stroke is an illness in which part of the brain is suddenly severely damaged or destroyed as a result of a blood clot or haemorrhage, leading to a loss of function of the affected part of the brain. If the clot is very big or affects a vital part of the brain, the patient may die. In less severe cases, partial or complete recovery occurs. In most cases, even when there is severe paralysis, there is no discernible effect on the intellect and memory, and the person's brain power is as good as ever. The effect on work therefore to a certain extent depends on the type of work formerly undertaken by the person.

Traumatic physical injuries, including head and spinal cord injuries, are one form of physical disability and are often the result of an accident. They can lead to minor and temporary impairments or more permanent and severe disablement. One difficulty is for people who were once physically active who have to readjust to a new lifestyle. Another is what has been described as a personality change which can affect the individual concerned and their family, friends and colleagues. Short-, medium- or long-term memory may also be affected.

For more information, see the addresses of specialist organizations in Appendix 4.

Appendix 2

The statute

DISABILITY RIGHTS COMMISSION ACT 1999

1999 Chapter 17

An Act to establish a Disability Rights Commission and make provision as to its functions; and for connected purposes.

[27th July 1999]

Be it enacted by the Queen's most Excellent Majesty, by and with the advice and consent of the Lords Spiritual and Temporal, and Commons, in this present Parliament assembled, and by the authority of the same, as follows:—

1.—(1) There shall be a body known as the Disability rights Commission (referred to in this Act as 'The Commission'). *The Disability Rights Commission.*

(2) The Secretary of State shall pay to the Commission such sums as he thinks fit to enable it to meet its expenses.

(3) Schedule 1 (the Commission's constitution and related matters) has effect.

(4) The National Disability Council (which is superseded by the Commission) is abolished.

2.—(1) The Commission shall have the following duties— *General Functions.*
   (a)   to work towards the elimination of discrimination against disabled persons;

(b) to promote the equalisation of opportunities for disabled persons;

(c) to take such steps as it considers appropriate with a view to encouraging good practice in the treatment of disabled persons; and

1995 c. 50.   (d) to keep under review the working of the Disability Discrimination Act 1995 (referred to in this Act as 'the 1995 Act') and this Act.

(2) The Commission may, for any purpose connected with the performance of its functions—

(a) make proposals or give other advice to any Minister of the Crown as to any aspect of the law or a proposed change to the law;

(b) make proposals or give other advice to any Government agency or other public authority as to the practical application of any law;

(c) undertake, or arrange for or support (whether financial or otherwise), the carrying out of research or the provision of advice or information.

Nothing in this subsection is to be regarded as limiting the Commission's powers.

(3) The Commission shall make proposals or give other advice under subsection (2)(a) on any matter specified in a request from a Minister of the Crown.

(4) The Commission may make charges for facilities or services made available by it for any purpose.

(5) In this section—

'disabled persons' includes persons who have had a disability;

'discrimination' means anything which is discrimination for the purposes of any provision of Part II or Part III of the 1995 Act; and

'the law' includes Community law and the international obligations of the United Kingdom.

Formal investigations.   **3.**—(1) The Commission may decide to conduct a formal investigation for any purpose connected with the performance of its duties under section 2(1).

(2) The Commission shall conduct a formal investigation if directed to do so by the Secretary of State for any such purpose.

(3) The Commission may at any time decide to stop or to suspend the conduct of a formal investigation; but any such decision requires the approval of the Secretary of State if the investigation is being conducted in pursuance of a direction under subsection (2).

(4) The Commission may, as respects any formal investigation which it has decided or been directed to conduct—

(a) nominate one or more commissioners, with or without one or more additional commissioners appointed for the purposes of the investigation, to conduct the investigation on its behalf; and

(b) authorise those persons to exercise such of its functions in relation to the investigation (which may include drawing up or revising terms of reference) as it may determine.

(5) Schedule 2 (appointment and tenure of office of additional commissioners) and Schedule 3 (so far as relating to the conduct of formal investigations) have effect.

4.—(1) If in the course of a formal investigation the Commission is satisfied that a person has committed or is committing an unlawful act, it may serve on him a notice (referred to in this Act as a non-discrimination notice) which— Non-discrimination notices.

(a) gives details of the unlawful act which the Commission has found that he has committed or is committing; and

(b) requires him not to commit any further unlawful acts of the same kind (and, if the finding is that he is committing an unlawful act, to cease doing so).

(2) The notice may include recommendations to the person concerned as to action which the Commission considers he could reasonably be expected to take with a view to complying with the requirement mentioned in subsection (1)(b).

(3) The notice may require the person concerned—

(a) to propose an adequate action plan (subject to and in accordance with Part III of Schedule 3) with a

163

view to securing compliance with the requirement mentioned in subsection (1)(b); and

(b) once an action plan proposed by him has become final, to take any action which—
(i) is specified in the plan; and
(ii) he has not already taken,
at the time or times specified in the plan.

(4) For the purposes of subsection (3)—

(a) an action plan is a document drawn up by the person concerned specifying action (including action he has already taken) intended to change anything in his practices, policies, procedures or other arrangements which—
(i) caused or contributed to the commission of the unlawful act concerned; or
(ii) is liable to cause or contribute to a failure to comply with the requirement mentioned in subsection (1)(b); and

(b) an action plan is adequate if the action specified in it would be sufficient to ensure, within a reasonable time, that he is not prevented from complying with that requirement by anything in his practices, policies, procedures or other arrangements;

and the action specified in an action plan may include ceasing an activity or taking continuing action over a period.

(5) In this section 'unlawful act' means an act which is unlawful discrimination for the purposes of any provision of Part II or Part III of the 1995 Act or any other unlawful act of a description prescribed for the purposes of this section.

(6) Schedule 3 (so far as relating to non-discrimination notices and action plans) has effect.

Agreements in lieu of enforcement action.

5.—(1) If the Commission has reason to believe that a person has committed or is committing an unlawful act, it may (subject to section 3(3)) enter into an agreement in writing under this section with that person on the assumption that that belief is well founded (whether or not that person admits that he committed or is committing the act in question).

(2) An agreement under this section is one by which—
  (a) the Commission undertakes not to take any relevant enforcement action in relation to the unlawful act in question; and
  (b) the person concerned undertakes—
    (i) not to commit any further unlawful acts of the same kind (and, where appropriate, to cease committing the unlawful act in question); and
    (ii) to take such action (which may include ceasing an activity or taking continuing action over any period) as may be specified in the agreement.

(3) Those undertakings are binding on the parties to the agreement; but undertakings under subsection (2)(b) are enforceable by the Commission only as provided by subsection (8).

(4) For the purposes of subsection (2)(a), 'relevant enforcement' means—
  (a) beginning a formal investigation into the commission by the person concerned of the unlawful act in question;
  (b) if such an investigation has begun (whether or not the investigation is confined to that matter), taking any further steps in the investigation of that matter; and
  (c) taking any steps, or further steps, with a view to the issue of a non-discrimination notice based on the commission of the unlawful act in question.

(5) The action specified in an undertaking under subsection (2)(b)(ii) must be action intended to change anything in the practices, policies, procedures or other arrangements of the person concerned which—
  (a) caused or contributed to the commission of the unlawful act in question; or
  (b) is liable to cause or contribute to a failure to comply with his undertaking under subsection (2)(b)(i).

(6) An agreement under this section—
  (a) may include terms providing for incidental or supplementary matter (including the termination of the agreement, or the right of either party to terminate it, in certain circumstances); and

(b) may be varied or revoked by agreement of the parties.

(7) An agreement under this section may not include any provisions other than terms mentioned in subsections (2) and (6)(a) unless their inclusion is authorised by regulations made by the Secretary of State for the purposes of this section; but any provisions so authorised are not enforceable by the Commission under subsection (8).

(8) The Commission may apply to a county court or by summary application to the sheriff for an order under this subsection if—
  (a) the other party to an agreement under this section has failed to comply with any undertaking under subsection (2)(b); or
  (b) the Commission has reasonable cause to believe that he intends not to comply with any such undertaking.

(9) An order under subsection (8) is an order requiring the other party to comply with the undertaking or with such directions for the same purpose as are contained in the order.

(10) Nothing in this section affects the Commission's powers to settle or compromise legal proceedings of any description.

(11) In this section 'unlawful act' means an act which is unlawful discrimination for the purposes of any provision of Part II or Part III of the 1995 Act or any other unlawful act of a description prescribed for the purposes of this section.

(12) Schedule 3 (so far as relating to agreements under this section) has effect.

Persistent discrimination.

6.—(1) This section applies during the period of five years beginning on the date on which—
  (a) a non-discrimination notice served on a person,
  (b) a finding by a court or tribunal in proceedings under section 8 or 25 of the 1995 Act that a person has committed an act which is unlawful discrimination for the purposes of any provision of Part II or Part III of that Act, or

(c) a finding by a court or tribunal in any other proceedings that a person has committed an act of a description prescribed under subsection (4)(b),

has become final.

(2) If during that period it appears to the Commission that unless restrained the person concerned is likely to do one or more unlawful acts, the Commission may apply to a county court for an injunction, or to the sheriff for interdict, restraining him from doing so.

(3) The court, if satisfied that the application is well-founded, may grant the injunction or interdict in the terms applied for or in more limited terms.

(4) In this section 'unlawful act' means an act which is unlawful discrimination for the purposes of any provision of Part II or Part III of the 1995 Act or any other unlawful act of a description prescribed for the purposes of this section.

(5) A finding of a court or tribunal becomes final for the purposes of this section when an appeal against it is dismissed, withdrawn or abandoned or when the time for appealing expires without an appeal having been brought.

7.—(1) This section applies to— Assistance in relation to proceedings.

    (a) proceedings which an individual has brought or proposes to bring under section 8 or 25 of the 1995 Act (complaints and claims about unlawful discrimination under Parts II and III); and

    (b) proceedings of a description prescribed for the purposes of this subsection, being proceedings in which an individual who has or has had a disability relies or proposes to rely on a matter relating to that disability.

(2) Where the individual concerned applies to the Commission for assistance in relation to any proceedings to which this section applies, the Commission may grant the application on any of the following grounds—

    (a) that the case raises a question of principle;

    (b) that it is unreasonable to expect the applicant to deal with the case unaided (because of its complexity, because of the applicant's position in relation to another party or for some other reason);

(c) that there is some other special consideration which makes it appropriate for the Commission to provide assistance.

(3) If the Commission grants an application, it may—

(a) provide or arrange for the provision of legal advice;

(b) arrange for legal or other representation (which may include any assistance usually given by a solicitor or counsel);

(c) seek to procure the settlement of any dispute;

(d) provide or arrange for the provision of any other assistance which it thinks appropriate.

(4) Subsection (3)(b) does not affect the law and practice as to who may represent a person in relation to any proceedings.

(5) The Commission may authorise any employee of the Commission to exercise such of its functions under this section as it may determine.

Recovery of expenses of providing assistance.

8.—(1) This section applies where—

(a) the Commission has given an individual assistance under section 7 in relation to any proceedings; and

(b) any costs or expenses (however described) have become payable to him by another person in respect of the matter in connection with which the assistance is given.

(2) A sum equal to any expenses incurred by the Commission in providing the assistance shall be a first charge for the benefit of the Commission on the costs or expenses concerned.

(3) It is immaterial for the purposes of this section whether the costs or expenses concerned are payable by virtue of a decision of a court or tribunal, an agreement arrived at to avoid proceedings or to bring them to an end, or otherwise.

(4) The charge created by this section is subject to—

1988 c. 34.

(a) any charge under the Legal Aid Act 1988 and any provision in that Act for payment of any sum to the Legal Aid Board; and

(b) any charge or obligation for payment in priority to other debts under the Legal Aid (Scotland) Act 1986 and any provision in that Act for payment 1986 c. 47. of any sum into the Scottish Legal Aid Fund.

(5) Provision may be made by regulations made by the Secretary of State for the determination of the expenses of the Commission in cases where this section applies.

9.—(1) The following section shall be inserted at the Codes of beginning of Part VII of the 1995 Act (supple- practice. mental)—

53A.—(1) The Disability Rights Commission may prepare and issue codes of practice giving practical guidance—

(a) to employers, service providers or other persons to whom provisions of Part II or Part III apply on how to avoid discrimination or on any other matter relating to the operation of those provisions in relation to them; or

(b) to any persons on any other matter, with a view to—

(i) promoting the equalisation of opportunities for disabled persons and persons who have had a disability, or

(ii) encouraging good practice regarding the treatment of such persons,

in any field of activity regulated by any provision of Part II or Part III.

(2) The Commission shall, when requested to do so by the Secretary of State, prepare a code of practice dealing with the matters specified in the request.

(3) In preparing a code of practice the Commission shall carry out such consultations as it considers appropriate (which shall include the publication for public consultation of proposals relating to the code).

(4) The Commission may not issue a code of practice unless—

(a) a draft of it has been submitted to and approved by the Secretary of State and laid by him before both Houses of Parliament; and

(b) the 40 day period has elapsed without either House resolving not to approve the draft.

(5) If the Secretary of State does not approve a draft code of practice submitted to him he shall give the Commission a written statement of his reasons.

(6) A code of practice issued by the Commission—
   (a) shall come into effect on such day as the Secretary of State may by order appoint;
   (b) may be revised in whole or part, and re-issued, by the Commission; and
   (c) may be revoked by an order made by the Secretary of State at the request of the Commission.

(7) Where the Commission proposes to revise a code of practice—
   (a) it shall comply with subsection (3) in relation to the revisions; and
   (b) the other provisions of this section apply to the revised code of practice as they apply to a new code of practice.

(8) Failure to observe any provision of a code of practice does not of itself make a person liable to any proceedings, but any provision of a code which appears to a court or tribunal to be relevant to any question arising in any proceedings under Part II or Part III shall be taken into account in determining that question.

(9) In this section—

'code of practice' means a code of practice under this section;
'discrimination' means anything which is unlawful discrimination for the purposes of any provision of Part II or Part III; and
'40 day period' has the same meaning in relation to a draft code of practice as it has in section 3 in rela tion to draft guidance.'

(2) The Commission may treat any consultation undertaken by the National Disability Council under section 52(2) of the 1995 Act as being as effective for the purposes of section 53A(3) of that Act as if it had been undertaken by the Commission.

(3) Nothing in this section affects the Commission's powers apart from this section to give practical guidance on matters connected with its functions.

10. For section 28 of the 1995 Act (arrangements by the Secretary of State with a view to the settlement of disputes under Part III) there shall be substituted the following section— Conciliation of disputes under Part III of the 1995 Act.

28.—(1) The Commission may make arrangements with any other person for the provision of conciliation services by, or by persons appointed by, that person in relation to disputes arising under this Part. Conciliation of disputes.

(2) In deciding what arrangements (if any) to make, the Commission shall have regard to the desirability of securing, so far as reasonably practicable, that conciliation services are available for all disputes arising under this Part which the parties may wish to refer to conciliation.

(3) No member or employee of the Commission may provide conciliation services in relation to disputes arising under this Part.

(4) The Commission shall ensure that any arrangements under this section include appropriate safeguards to prevent the disclosure to members or employees of the Commission of information obtained by a person in connection with the provision of conciliation services in pursuance of the arrangements.

(5) Subsection (4) does not apply to information relating to a dispute which is disclosed with the consent of the parties to that dispute.

(6) Subsection (4) does not apply to information which—
   (a) is not identifiable with a particular dispute or a particular person; and
   (b) is reasonably required by the Commission for the purpose of monitoring the operation of the arrangements concerned.

(7) Anything communicated to a person while providing conciliation services in pursuance of any arrangements under this section is not admissible in evidence in any proceedings except with the consent of the person who communicated it to that person.

(8) In this section 'conciliation services' means advice and assistance provided by a conciliator to the parties to a dispute with a view to promoting its settlement otherwise than through the courts'.

Procedure for amending s.7(1) of the 1995 Act.

11. For subsections (3) to (10) of section 7 of the 1995 Act (exemption for small business) there shall be substituted the following subsections—

'(3) Before making an order under subsection (2) the Secretary of State shall consult—
(a) the Disability Rights Commission;
(b) such organisations representing the interests of employers as he considers appropriate; and
(c) such organisations representing the interests of disabled persons in employment or seeking employment as he considers appropriate.

(4) The Secretary of State shall, before laying an order under this section before Parliament, publish a summary of the views expressed to him in his consultations.'

Regulations.

12.—(1) Any power under this Act to make regulations is exercisable by statutory instrument.

(2) Any such regulations may make—
(a) different provision for different case or areas;
(b) provision enabling a person to exercise a discretion in dealing with any matter; and
(c) incidental, supplemental, consequential or transitional provision.

(3) A statutory instrument containing any such regulations shall be subject to annulment in pursuance of a resolution of either House or Parliament.

13.—(1) In this Act—

Interpretation.

'Commission' means the Disability Rights Commission;

'final', in relation to a non-discrimination notice, has the meaning given by paragraph 11 of Schedule 3;

'formal investigation' means an investigation under section 3;

'non-discrimination notice' means a notice under section 4;

'notice' means notice in writing;

'prescribed' means prescribed in regulations made by the Secretary of State; and

'the 1995 Act' means the Disability Discrimination Act 1995. 1995 c. 50.

(2) Expressions used in this Act which are defined for the purposes of the 1995 Act have the same meaning in this Act as in that Act.

14.—(1) Schedule 4 (minor and consequential amendments) has effect. Consequential amendments and repeals.

(2) The enactments mentioned in Schedule 5 are repealed to the extent specified.

15. This Act binds the Crown (but does not affect Her Majesty in her private capacity or in right of Her Duchy of Lancaster or the Duke of Cornwall). Crown applications.

16.—(1) This Act may be cited as the Disability Rights Commission Act 1999. Short title, commencement and extent.

(2) This Act (apart from this section) shall come into force on such day as the Secretary of State may by order made by statutory instrument appoint; and different days may be appointed for different purposes.

(3) An order under subsection (2) may contain transitional provisions and savings relating to the provisions brought into force by the order.

(4) The following provisions extend to Northern Ireland—
    (a) section 14(1), in relation to paragraphs 1, 2 and 4 of Schedule 4; and
    (b) section 14(2), in relation to the repeal of words in the House of Commons Disqualification Act 1975, the Northern Ireland Assembly Disqualification Act 1975 and section 70(7) of the 1995 Act. 1975 c. 24. 1975 c. 25.

(5) Except as mentioned in subsection (4), this Act does not extend to Northern Ireland.

SCHEDULES

Section 1(3).

SCHEDULE 1
CONSTITUTION ETC

Status

1.—(1) the Commission is a body corporate.

(2) The Commission is not the servant or agent of the Crown, it does not enjoy any status, immunity or privilege of the Crown and its property is not to be regarded as property of or as held on behalf of the Crown.

Membership

2.—(1) The Commission shall consist of not less than 10 and not more than 15 commissioners appointed by the Secretary of State.

(2) The Secretary of State may appoint as a commissioner a person who is not disabled and has not had a disability only if satisfied that after the appointment more than half of the commissioners will be disabled persons or persons who have had a disability.

(3) Sub-paragraph (2) shall not apply in respect of the first three appointments under this paragraph.

Tenure of office of commissioners

3.—(1) A commissioner shall hold and vacate office in accordance with the terms of his appointment.

(2) A person shall not be appointed a commissioner for less than two or more than five years; but a person who has served as a commissioner may be reappointed.

4. A commissioner may resign by notice in writing to the Secretary of State.

5. The Secretary of State may terminate the appointment of a commissioner if satisfied that—
   (a) without the consent of the chairman he has failed to attend meetings of the Commission during a continuous period of six months beginning not earlier than nine months before the termination;

(b) he has become bankrupt, has had his estate sequestrated or has made a composition or arrangement
with, or granted a trust deed for, his creditors; or

(c) he is otherwise unable or unfit to carry out his
functions as a commissioner.

Tenure of office of chairman and deputy chairmen

6.—(1) The Secretary of State shall appoint one commissioner as chairman of the Commission and either one
or two other commissioners as deputy chairmen.

(2) The Secretary of State shall exercise his powers of
appointment under this paragraph with a view to
securing that at least one of the persons holding office
as chairman or deputy chairman is a disabled person
or a person who has had a disability.

7. A person appointed as chairman or deputy chairman—
(a) shall hold and vacate that office in accordance with
the terms of his appointment,
(b) may resign that office by notice in writing to the
Secretary of State, and
(c) shall cease to hold that office if he ceases to be a
commissioner.

Remuneration, pensions etc. of commissioners

8. The Commission may—
(a) pay to any commissioner such remuneration or
expenses; and
(b) pay, or make provision for the payment of, such
sums by way of pensions, allowances or gratuities
to or in respect of any commissioner, as the
Secretary of State may determine.

9. If the Secretary of State determines that there are
special circumstances which make it right that a person
who has ceased to be a commissioner should receive
compensation, the Secretary of State may direct the
Commission to pay that person such sum by way of
compensation as the Secretary of State may determine.

Staff

10.—(1) The Commission shall have—
(a) a chief executive appointed by the Commission,

subject to the approval of the Secretary of State; and

(b) such other employees as the Commission may appoint, subject to the approval of the Secretary of State as to numbers and terms and conditions of service.

(2) The first appointment of a chief executive shall be made by the Secretary of State.

1972 c. 11.   11.—(1) Employment with the Commission shall be included among the kinds of employment to which a scheme under section 1 of the Superannuation Act 1972 may apply, and accordingly in Schedule 1 to that Act (in which those kinds of employment are listed) at the end of the list of Royal Commissioners and other Commissions there shall be inserted—

'Disability Rights Commission.'

(2) The Commission shall pay to the Minister for the Civil Service, at such times as he may direct, such sums as he may determine in respect of the increase attributable to sub-paragraph (1) in the sums payable out of money provided by Parliament under that Act.

Proceedings etc.

12.—(1) The Commission may regulate its own procedure (including quorum).

(2) The quorum for meetings of the Commission shall in the first instance be determined by a meeting of the Commission attended by at least five commissioners.

13. The validity of any proceedings of the Commission is not affected by a vacancy among the commissioners or by a defect in the appointment of a commissioner.

Delegation

14.—(1) The Commission may authorise any committee of the Commission or any commissioner to exercise such of its functions (other than functions relating to the conduct of a formal investigation) as it may determine.

(2) This paragraph does not affect any power of the Commission to authorise its employees to do anything on its behalf.

Accounts

15.—(1) The Commission shall—
  (a) keep proper accounts and proper records in relation to the accounts,
  (b) prepare a statement of accounts in respect of each accounting year, and
  (c) send copies of the statement to the Secretary of State and the Comptroller and Auditor General not later than the 31st August following the end of the accounting year to which it relates.

(2) The Comptroller and Auditor General shall examine, certify and report on the statement of accounts and shall lay copies of the statement and of his report before each House of Parliament.

(3) The Commission's accounting year is the twelve months dealing with 31st March.

(4) The Commission's first accounting year shall be the period of not more than 12 months beginning with the Commission's establishment and ending with 31st March.

Annual reports

16.—(1) As soon as practicable after the end of each accounting year the Commission shall submit to the Secretary of State a report on its activities during that year.

(2) The report shall include (among other things)—
  (a) a report on anything done by the Commission, in the performance of its functions under section 2(1)(a) to (c), jointly or otherwise in cooperation with any other organisation;
  (b) a general survey of developments in matters within the scope of the Commission's functions; and
  (c) proposals for the Commission's activities in the current year.

(3) The Secretary of State shall lay a copy of the report before Parliament and arrange for such further publication of it as he considers appropriate.

List of consultees

17.—(1) The Commission shall maintain a list of the organisations it has consulted generally for the purposes of any of its functions.

(2) An organisation may be removed from the list if it has not been consulted generally in the 12 months preceding its removal.

(3) For the purposes of sub-paragraphs (1) and (2), consultation is general unless it relates only—
  (a) to an investigation to which paragraph 3 of Schedule 3 applies,
  (b) to assistance under section 7, or
  (c) otherwise to a particular individual or individ uals.

(4) The Commission shall make the list available to the public in whatever way it considers appropriate (subject to any charge it may impose).

SCHEDULE 2
Section 3(5).
ADDITIONAL COMMISSIONERS

1.—(1) The Commission may, with the approval of the Secretary of State, appoint one or more individuals as additional commissioners for the purposes of a formal investigation.

(2) An additional commissioner is not the servant or agent of the Crown.

2.—(1) An additional commissioner shall hold and vacate office in accordance with the terms of his appointment (and may be re-appointed).

(2) The Commission may not alter the terms of appointment of an additional commissioner except with his consent and the approval of the Secretary of State.

3. The Commission may—
  (a) pay such remuneration or expenses to any additional commissioner as the Secretary of State may determine, and
  (b) pay, or make provision for the payment of, such sums by way of pensions, allowances or gratuities to or in respect of any additional commissioner as the Secretary of State may determine.

4.—(1) An additional commissioner may resign by notice in writing to the Commission.

(2) The Commission may, with the approval of the Secretary of State, terminate the appointment of an additional commissioner if satisfied that—

(a) without reasonable excuse he has failed to carry out his duties during a continuous period of three months beginning not earlier than six months before the termination;

(b) he has become bankrupt, has had his estate sequestrated or has made a composition or arrangement with, or granted a trust deed for, his creditors; or

(c) he is otherwise unable or unfit to carry out his duties.

(3) The appointment of an additional commissioner shall otherwise terminate at the conclusion of the investigation for which he was appointed.

5. If the Secretary of State determines that there are special circumstances which make it right that a person who has ceased to be an additional commissioner should receive compensation, the Secretary of State may direct the Commission to pay that person such sum by way of compensation as the Secretary of State may determine.

SCHEDULE 3
FORMAL INVESTIGATIONS AND NON-DISCRIMINATION NOTICES

Sections 3(5), 4(6) and 5(12).

PART I
CONDUCT OF FORMAL INVESTIGATIONS

Introductory

1.—(1) This Part of this Schedule applies to a formal investigation which the Commission has decided or has been directed to conduct.

(2) Any subsequent action required or authorised by this Part of this Schedule (or by Part IV of this Schedule) to be taken by the Commission in relation to the conduct of a formal investigation may be taken, so far as they are authorised to do so, by persons nominated under section 3(4) for the purposes of the investigation.

Terms of reference and preliminary notices

2.—(1) The Commission shall not take any steps in the conduct of a formal investigation until—

(a) terms of reference for the investigation have been drawn up; and

(b) notice of the holding of the investigation and the terms of reference has been served or published as required by sub-paragraph (3) or (4).

(2) The terms of reference for the investigation shall be drawn up (and may be revised)—

(a) if the investigation is held at the direction of the Secretary of State, by the Secretary of State after consulting the Commission; and

(b) in any other case, by the Commission.

(3) Where the terms of reference confine the investigation to activities of one or more named persons, notice of the holding of the investigation and the terms of reference shall be served on each of those persons.

(4) Where the terms of reference do not confine the investigation to activities of one or more named persons, notice of the holding of the investigation and the terms of reference shall be published in such manner as appears to the Commission appropriate to bring it to the attention of persons likely to be affected by it.

(5) If the terms of reference are revised, this paragraph applies again in relation to the revised investigation and its terms of reference.

Investigation of unlawful acts etc.

3.—(1) This paragraph applies where the Commission proposes to investigate in the course of a formal investigation (whether or not the investigation has already begun) whether—

(a) a person has committed or is committing any unlawful act;

(b) any requirement imposed by a non-discrimination notice served on a person (including a requirement to take action specified in an action plan) has been or is being complied with;

(c) any undertaking given by a person in an agreement made with the Commission under section 5 is being or has been complied with.

(2) The Commission may not investigate any such matter unless the terms of reference of the investigation confine it to the activities of one or more named persons (and the person concerned is one of those persons).

(3) The Commission may not investigate whether a person has committed or is committing any unlawful act unless—
  (a) it has reason to believe that the person concerned may have committed or may be committing the act in question, or
  (b) that matter is to be investigated in the course of a formal investigation into his compliance with any requirement or undertaking mentioned in sub-paragraph (1)(b) or (c).

(4) The Commission shall serve a notice on the person concerned offering him the opportunity to make written and oral representations about the matters being investigated.

(5) If the Commission is investigating whether the person concerned has committed or is committing any unlawful act (otherwise than in the course of a formal investigation into his compliance with any requirement or undertaking mentioned in sub-paragraph (1)(b) or (c)) the Commission shall include in the notice required by sub-paragraph (4) a statement informing that person that the Commission has reason to believe that he may have committed or may be committing any unlawful act.

(6) The Commission shall not make any findings in relation to any matter mentioned in sub-paragraph (1) without giving the person concerned or his representative a reasonable opportunity to make written and oral representations.

(7) The Commission may refuse to receive oral representations made on behalf of the person concerned by a person (not being counsel or a solicitor) to whom the Commission reasonably objects as being unsuitable.

(8) If the Commission refuses to receive oral representations from a person under sub-paragraph (7), it shall give reasons in writing for its objection.

(9) A notice required by sub-paragraph (4) may be included in a notice required by paragraph 2(3).

(10) In this paragraph 'unlawful act' means an act which is unlawful discrimination for the purposes of any provision of Part II or Part III or the 1995 Act or any other unlawful act of a description prescribed for the purposes of this paragraph.

Power to obtain information

4.—(1) For the purposes of a formal investigation the Commission may serve a notice on any person requiring him—
   (a) to give such written information as may be described in the notice; or
   (b) to attend and give oral information about any matter specified in the notice, and to produce all documents in his possession or control relating to any such matter.

(2) A notice under this paragraph may only be served on the written authority of the Secretary of State unless the terms of reference confine the investigation to the activities of one or more named persons and the person being served is one of those persons.

(3) A person may not be required by a notice under this paragraph—
   (a) to give information, or produce a document, which he could not be compelled to give in evidence, or produce, in civil proceedings before the High Court or the Court of Session; or
   (b) to attend at any place unless the necessary expenses of his journey to and from that place are paid or tendered to him.

5.—(1) The Commission may apply to a county court or by summary application to the sheriff for an order under this paragraph if—
   (a) a person has been served with a notice under paragraph 4; and
   (b) he fails to comply with it or the Commission has reasonable cause to believe that he intends not to comply with it.

(2) An order under this paragraph is an order requiring the person concerned to comply with the notice or with such directions for the same purpose as may be contained in the order.

Recommendations

6.—(1) The Commission may make recommendations in the light of its findings in a formal investigation.

(2) The recommendations may be—
  (a) recommendations to any person for changes in his policies or procedures, or as to any other matter, with a view to promoting the equalisation of opportunities for disabled persons or persons who have had a disability, or
  (b) recommendations to the Secretary of State, for changes in the law or otherwise.

(3) The Commission may make such recommendations before the conclusion of the investigation concerned.

Reports

7.—(1) The Commission shall prepare a report of its findings in any formal investigation.

(2) The Commission shall exclude from such a report any matter which relates to an individual's private affairs or any person's business interests if—
  (a) publication of that matter might, in the Commission's opinion, prejudicially affect that individual or person, and
  (b) its exclusion is consistent with the Commission's duties and the object of the report.

(3) The report of an investigation carried out at the direction of the Secretary of State shall be published by the Secretary of State or, if the Secretary of State so directs, by the Commission.

(4) The report of any other investigation shall be published by the Commission.

(5) Nothing in this paragraph affects the Commission's power to issue a non-discrimination notice before a report is prepared or published.

PART II
NON-DISCRIMINATION NOTICES

Procedure for issuing and appealing against non-discrimination notices

8.—(1) The Commission shall not issue a non-discrimination notice addressed to any person unless it has complied with the requirements of this paragraph.

(2) The Commission shall serve on the person concerned a notice—
  (a) informing him that the Commission is considering issuing a non-discrimination notice and of the grounds for doing so,
  (b) offering him the opportunity to make written and oral representations.

(3) The Commission shall give the person concerned or his representative the opportunity of making oral and written representations within a period specified in the notice of not less than 28 days.

(4) The Commission may refuse to receive oral representations made on behalf of the person concerned by a person (not being counsel or a solicitor) to whom the Commission reasonably objects as being unsuitable.

(5) If the Commission refuses to receive oral representations from a person under sub-paragraph (4), it shall give reasons in writing for its objection.

9. On issuing a non-discrimination notice, the Commission shall serve a copy on the person to whom it is addressed.

Appeal against non-discrimination notice

10.—(1) A person on whom a non-discrimination notice is served may, within the period of six weeks beginning on the day after the day on which the notice is served on him, appeal against any requirement imposed by the notice under section 4(1)(b) or (3).

(2) An appeal under this paragraph lies—
  (a) to an employment tribunal, so far as the requirement relates to acts within the tribunal's jurisdiction; and

(b) to a county court or a sheriff court, so far as the requirement relates to acts which are not within the jurisdiction of an employment tribunal.

(3) The court or tribunal may quash or, in Scotland, recall any requirement appealed against—
   (a) if it considers the requirement to be unreasonable; or
   (b) in the case of a requirement imposed under section 4(1)(b), if it considers that the Commission's finding that the person concerned had committed or is committing the unlawful act in question was based on an incorrect finding of fact.

(4) On quashing or recalling a requirement, the court or tribunal may direct that the non-discrimination notice shall have effect with such modifications as it considers appropriate.

(5) The modifications which may be included in such a direction include—
   (a) the substitution of a requirement in different terms; and
   (b) in the case of a requirement imposed under section 4(1)(b), modifications to the details given under section 4(1)(a) so far as necessary to describe any unlawful act on which the requirement could properly have been based.

(6) Sub-paragraph (1) does not apply to any modifications contained in a direction under sub-paragraph (4).

(7) If the court or tribunal allows an appeal under this paragraph without quashing or recalling the whole of the non-discrimination notice, the Commission may by notice to the person concerned vary the non-discrimination notice—
   (a) by revoking or altering any recommendation included in pursuance of the Commission's power under section 4(2); or
   (b) by making new recommendations in pursuance of that power.

11. For the purposes of this Act a non-discrimination notice becomes final when—
   (a) an appeal under paragraph 10 is dismissed, withdrawn or abandoned or the time for appealing

expires without an appeal having been brought; or

(b) an appeal under that paragraph is allowed without the whole notice being quashed or, in Scotland, recalled.

Enforcement of non-discrimination notice

12.—(1) This paragraph applies during the period of five years beginning on the date on which a non-discrimination notice served on a person has become final.

(2) During that period the Commission may apply to a county court or by summary application to the sheriff for an order under this paragraph, if—

(a) it appears to the Commission that the person concerned has failed to comply with any requirement imposed by the notice under section 4(1)(b); or

(b) the Commission has reasonable cause to believe that he intends not to comply with any such requirement.

(3) An order under this paragraph is an order requiring the person concerned to comply with the requirement or with such directions for the same purpose as are contained in the order.

Register of non-discrimination notices

13.—(1) The Commission shall maintain a register of non-discrimination notices which have become final.

(2) The Commission shall, in the case of notices which impose a requirement to propose an action plan, note on the register the date on which any action plan proposed by the person concerned has become final.

(3) The Commission shall arrange for—

(a) the register to be available for inspection at all reasonable times, and

(b) certified copies of any entry to be provided if required by any person.

(4) The Commission shall publish those arrangements in such manner as it considers appropriate to bring them to the attention of persons likely to be interested.

PART III
ACTION PLANS

Introductory

14.—(1) This Part of this Schedule applies where a person ('P') has been served with a non-discrimination notice which has become final and includes a requirement for him to propose an action plan.

(2) In this Part 'adequate' in relation to a proposed action plan means adequate (as defined in section 4(4)(b)) for the purposes of the requirement mentioned in section 4(1)(b).

The first proposed action plan

15.—(1) P must serve his proposed action plan on the Commission within such period as may be specified in the non-discrimination notice.

(2) If P fails to do so, the Commission may apply to a county court or by way of summary application to the sheriff for an order directing him to serve his proposed action plan within such period as the order may specify.

(3) If P serves a proposed action plan on the Commission in response to the non-discrimination notice, or to an order under sub-paragraph (2), the action plan shall become final at the end of the prescribed period, unless the Commission has given notice to P under paragraph 16.

Revision of first proposed action plan at invitation of Commission

16.—(1) If the Commission considers that a proposed action plan served on it is not an adequate action plan, the Commission may give notice to P—
   (a) stating its view that the plan is not adequate; and
   (b) inviting him to serve on the Commission a revised action plan which is adequate, within such period as may be specified in the notice.

(2) A notice under this paragraph may include recommendations as to action which the Commission considers might be included in an adequate action plan.

(3) If P serves a revised proposed action plan on the Commission in response to a notice under this paragraph, it shall supersede the previous proposed action plan and become final at the end of the prescribed period, unless the Commission has applied for an order under paragraph 17.

(4) If P does not serve a revised action plan in response to a notice under this paragraph, the action plan previously served on the Commission shall become final at the end of the prescribed period, unless the Commission has applied for an order under paragraph 17.

Action by Commission as respects inadequate action plan

17.—(1) If the Commission considers that a proposed action plan served on it is not an adequate action plan it may apply to the county court or by way of summary application to the sheriff for an order under this paragraph.

(2) The Commission may not make an application under this paragraph in relation to the first proposed action plan served on it by P (even where it was served in compliance with an order of the court under paragraph 15(2)) unless—
  (a) a notice under paragraph 16 has been served on P in relation to that proposed action plan; and
  (b) P has not served a revised action plan on the Commission in response to it within the period specified in the notice under paragraph 16(1)(b).

(3) An order under this paragraph is an order—
  (a) declaring that the proposed action plan in question is not an adequate action plan;
  (b) requiring P to revise his proposals and serve on the Commission an adequate action plan within such period as the order may specify; and
  (c) containing such directions (if any) as the court considers appropriate as to the action which should be specified in the adequate action plan required by the order.

(4) If on an application under this paragraph the court does not make an order, the proposed action plan in

question shall become final at the end of the prescribed period.

18.—(1) This paragraph applies where an order of the court under paragraph 17 ('the order') requires P to serve an adequate action plan on the Commission.

(2) If, in response to the order, P serves an action plan on the Commission, that action plan shall become final at the end of the prescribed period unless the Commission has applied to a county court or, in Scotland, to the sheriff to enforce the order on the ground that the plan does not comply with the order (and any directions under paragraph 17(3)(c)).

(3) where an application is made as mentioned in sub-paragraph (2)—
   (a) if the Commission withdraws its application, the action plan in question shall become final at the end of the prescribed period;
   (b) if the court considers that the action plan in question complies with the order, that action plan shall become final at the end of the prescribed period.

Variation of action plans

19. An action plan which has become final may be varied by agreement in writing between the Commission and P.

Enforcement of action plans

20.—(1) This paragraph applies during the period of five years beginning on the date on which an action plan drawn up by P becomes final.

(2) If during that period the Commission considers that P has failed to comply with the requirement under section 4(3)(b) to carry out any action specified in the action plan, the Commission may apply to a county court or by summary application to the sheriff for an order under this paragraph.

(3) An order under this paragraph is an order requiring P to comply with that requirement or with such directions for the same purpose as are contained in the order.

Power to obtain information

21.—(1) For the purposes of determining whether—
  (a) an action plan proposed by P is an adequate action plan; or
  (b) P has complied or is complying with the requirement to take the action specified in an action plan which has become final,

the Commission may serve a notice on any person requiring him to give such information in writing, or copies of documents in his possession or control, relating to those matters as may be described in the notice.

(2) A person may not be required by a notice under this paragraph to give information, or produce a document, which he could not be compelled to give in evidence or produce in civil proceedings before the High Court or the Court of Session.

(3) The Commission may apply to a county court or by summary application to the sheriff for an order under this sub-paragraph if a person has been served with a notice under this paragraph and fails to comply with it.

(4) An order under sub-paragraph (3) is an order requiring the person concerned to comply with the notice or with such directions for the same purpose as may be contained in the order.

PART IV
SUPPLEMENTARY

Restriction on disclosure of information

22.—(1) No information given to the Commission by any person ('the informant') in connection with—
  (a) a formal investigation; or
  (b) the exercise of any of its functions in relation to non-discrimination notices, action plans and agreements under section 5,

shall be disclosed by the Commission or by any person who is or has been a commissioner, an additional commissioner or an employee of the Commission.

(2) Sub-paragraph (1) does not apply to any disclosure made—

(a) on the order of a court,

(b) with the informant's consent,

(c) in the form of a summary or other general statement published by the Commission which does not identify the informant or any other person to whom the information relates,

(d) in a report of the investigation published by the Commission,

(e) to a commissioner, an additional commissioner or an employee of the Commission, or, so far as is necessary for the proper performance of the Commission's functions, to other persons, or

(f) for the purpose of any civil proceedings to which the Commission is a party, or of any criminal proceedings.

(3) A person who discloses information contrary to sub-paragraph (1) is guilty of an offence and liable on summary conviction to a fine not exceeding level 5 on the standard scale.

Enforcement of court orders

23.—(1) This paragraph applies to any order made by a county court or the sheriff under section 5(8) or under any provision of this Schedule.

(2) Section 55 of the County Courts Act 1984 (penalty 1984 c. 28. for failure to give evidence) shall have effect in relation to a failure to comply with an order made by a county court to which this paragraph applies with the following modifications—

(a) for subsection (1) there shall be substituted—
'(1) Any person who fails without reasonable excuse to comply with an order made by a county court under section 5(8) of or any provision of Schedule 3 to the Disability Rights Commission Act 1999 shall forfeit such fine as the judge may direct.';

(b) subsection (3) shall be omitted (but without prejudice to the operation of paragraph 4(3)(b) of this Schedule); and

(c) in subsection (4), for the words 'the party injured by the refusal or neglect' there shall be substituted the words 'the Disability Rights Commission for expenses incurred or wasted in consequence of the failure to comply with the order concerned'.

(3) Where the sheriff finds a person to be in contempt of court in respect of the failure of a person to comply with an order made by the sheriff to which this paragraph applies—

1981 c. 49.

(a) notwithstanding section 15 of the Contempt of Court Act 1981, the sheriff shall not commit the person to prison; and

(b) the sheriff may grant decree in favour of the Commission for such amount of any fine imposed for the contempt as appears to the sheriff to be appropriate in respect of the expense incurred or wasted by the Commission (including the expenses of any proceedings under this Schedule) in consequence of the failure to comply with the order.

(4) If the Commission applies to a county court or, in Scotland, to the sheriff to enforce an order to which this paragraph applies, the court may modify the order.

Offences

24.—(1) A person who—

(a) deliberately alters, suppresses, conceals or destroys a document to which a notice under paragraph 4 or 21, or an order under paragraph 5 or 21(3), relates; or

(b) in complying with—
(i) a notice under paragraph 4 or 21;
(ii) a non-discrimination notice;
(iii) an agreement under section 5; or
(iv) an order of a court under section 5(8) or under any provision of this Schedule,

makes any statement which he knows to be false or misleading in a material particular or recklessly makes a statement which is false or misleading in a material particular, is guilty of an offence and liable on summary conviction to a fine not exceeding level 5 on the standard scale.

(2) Proceedings for an offence under this paragraph may (without prejudice to any jurisdiction exercisable apart from this sub-paragraph) be instituted—
  (a) against any person at any place at which he has an office or other place of business;
  (b) against an individual at any place where he resides, or at which he is for the time being.

Service of notices

25.—(1) Any notice required or authorised by any provision of this Schedule to be served on a person may be served by delivering it to him, by leaving it at his proper address or by sending it by post to him at that address.

(20) Any such notice may—
  (a) in the case of a body corporate, be served on the secretary or clerk of that body;
  (b) in the case of a partnership, be served on any partner or a person having control or management of the partnership business;
  (c) in the case of an unincorporated association (other than a partnership), may be served on any member of its governing body.

(3) For the purposes of this paragraph and section 7 of the Interpretation Act 1978 (service of documents) in its application to this paragraph, the proper address of any person is— 1978 c. 30.
  (a) in the case of a body corporate, its secretary or clerk, the address of its registered or principal office in the United Kingdom;
  (b) in the case of an unincorporated association (other than a partnership) or a member of its governing body, its principal office in the United Kingdom;
  (c) in any other case, his usual or last-known address (whether of his residence or of a place where he carries on business or is employed).

Regulations

26. The Secretary of State may make regulations making provision—

(a) supplementing Part I or II of this Schedule in connection with any matter concerned with the conduct of formal investigations or the procedures for issuing non-discrimination notices; or

(b) amending Part III of this Schedule in relation to the procedures for finalising action plans.

Section 14(1).

SCHEDULE 4
MINOR AND CONSEQUENTIAL AMENDMENTS

House of Commons Disqualification Act 1975 (c. 25)

1. In Part II of Schedule 1 to the House of Commons Disqualification Act 1975 (bodies whose members are disqualified) there shall be inserted at the appropriate place the words 'The Disability Rights Commission'.

Northern Ireland Assembly Disqualification Act 1975 (c. 26)

2. In Part II of Schedule 1 to the Northern Ireland Assembly Disqualification Act 1975 (bodies whose members are disqualified) there shall be inserted at the appropriate place the words 'The Disability Rights Commission'.

Disability Discrimination Act 1995 (c. 50)

3.—(1) The Disability Discrimination Act 1995 shall be amended as follows.

(2) In section 67(5) (orders not subject to annulment) for '52(8), 54(6)' substitute '53A(6)(a)'.

(3) In Schedule 3 (enforcement and procedure under Parts II and III), in paragraph 6(2), for the words from 'a person' to 'approached' there shall be substituted 'the dispute concerned is referred for conciliation in pursuance of arrangements under section 28'.

Scotland Act 1988 (c. 46)

4. In part III of Schedule 5 to the Scotland Act 1998 (reserved bodies), in paragraph 3(2)(c), for the words 'the National Disability Council' there shall be substituted 'the Disability Rights Commission'.

SCHEDULE 5
REPEALS

Section
14(2).

Chapter	Short title	Extent of repeal
1975 c. 24.	House of Commons Disqualification Act 1975.	In Part II of Schedule 1, the entry relating to the National Disability Council.
1975 c. 25.	Northern Ireland Assembly Disqualification Act 1975.	In Part II of Schedule 1, the entry relating to the National Disability Council.
1995 c. 50.	Disability Discrimination Act 1995.	Sections 50 to 54. In section 70(7), the words 'The National Disability Council'. Schedule 5.

Appendix 3

Providing access
for all

We include here some detail on building specifications with regard to people with disabilities, and follow this with a checklist for you to use in assessing the accessibility of your organization. This is really just basic guidance; for more information contact: The Centre for Accessible Environments, 60 Gainsford Street, London SE1 2NY, Tel: 0171 357 8182. The sources we used are: *Code of Practice for Access for the Disabled to Buildings* BS 5810: 1979, and *The Building Regulations 1985 Access for Disabled People.*

Please note that this section is primarily concerned with the provision of physical access. You are also advised to take into consideration such issues as access to information.

BUILDING SPECIFICATIONS

The following guidelines should be used to ensure that buildings are accessible to all.

External planning

Car parking. Reserved car parking spaces for people with disabilities should be sited nearest the entrance which they are likely to use on a regular basis. Reserved spaces should be clearly signposted and the ground should also be clearly marked.

The standard width of a parking bay is 2400mm. The recommended width to allow a driver or passenger with a disability to have easy movement into and out of the car is 3000mm.

The ground should be as level as possible.

Approach. Dropped kerbs are necessary. In places where movement has to be made from roadways to pavement the surfaces concerned should merge and the resulting gradient should not exceed 1 in 10.

Entrance to the building. The approach to at least one entrance from the adjacent street or car parking area should be level or ramped. Where ramped the gradient should not exceed 1 in 12. The width of the ramp should not be less than 1200mm and a handrail should be provided at both sides.

Where there are external steps, these should be edged in yellow and white and where possible be under cover. The step rise should be no more than 150mm, should be uniform and the tread width should not be less than 320mm. The total rise of any flight of consecutive steps should not exceed 1200mm. Top and bottom landings should have a textured surface to be easily identified by people with a visual impairment.

Entrance door. At least one door should give a clear opening width of not less than 800mm. Automatic sliding doors operated by a contact mat, or a radar or sonar detector, are preferable. Any glass doors should be clearly marked to indicate their presence. Where there are revolving doors, an ordinary door which satisfies the size requirement should be fitted close by. Where there is a lobby area, there should be sufficient space to allow a wheelchair user fully to clear one door before using the next.

Internal planning

What you do within the building needs to mesh with fire regulations.

Corridors/passageways. Corridors should be at least 1200mm wide, preferably a minimum of 1500mm for wheelchair users.

Internal doors. Internal doors should give a clear opening of at least 800mm. A glazed vision panel will allow people approaching from either side to have a clear view. Wherever possible, doors should open both ways. Glazed doors should be clearly marked to indicate their presence.

Door handles should be easy to hold and operate: a level handle is preferable to a knob. The handle should be fitted approximately

1040mm above floor level. A horizontal rail is easier for most people (especially wheelchair users) to grasp, rather than a short vertical handle.

Tension on spring closure should be reduced as far as is acceptable to allow people with less ability to grip and, particularly wheelchair users, to be able to open the doors without help.

Internal staircases. The step rise of an internal staircase should not exceed 170mm to allow full use of crutches. The tread width (known as 'goings') should be no less than 250mm and should be uniform. Tread surfaces should be non-slip. The total rise of the staircase should not exceed 1800mm.

Handrails should be provided at an overall height of approximately 1000mm from floor or landing level and should be easy to grip. If handrails are circular, a diameter of between 45mm and 50mm is preferred with a clearance at least 45mm from the wall. The handrails should be securely fastened as people with balance difficulties put a lot of strain on the handrails (and also to comply with the Health and Safety at Work etc Act).

The first and last steps in the flight should be of a contrasting colour to the rest.

Lifts. At entrance level the lift landing floor should be at the same level as an entrance door.

The clear space in front of lift doors should not be less than 1500mm × 1500mm. Lift doors should give a clear opening of at least 800mm, should stay open for a minimum of five seconds and should re-open if they meet with an obstruction when closing.

Standard size wheelchairs need minimum depth of the lift car of 1400mm and width not less than 1100mm.

Control buttons should be between 1000mm and 1400mm from floor level and should be identifiable by someone with a visual impairment. A telephone should be installed at a similar height.

Handrails should be fitted to the interior about 1000mm from the floor.

Public telephones. At least one telephone should be fixed at a lower level (not higher than 1400mm) to serve wheelchair users, and with a fold-down seat alongside for use by others who may have difficulty standing. One telephone should be fitted with amplifiers to assist people with impaired hearing.

Toilets. At least one toilet should be available with the compartment planned to allow a person to move, or be helped to move, from a wheelchair either frontally or horizontally on to the toilet. The door should open out or slide, except that an inward opening side hung door is permissible where there is sufficient unobstructed space (minimum 1100mm × 700mm) inside the WC compartment for a wheelchair to be positioned clear of the line of the door swing. Vertical and horizontal support rails should be provided beside the toilet. The toilet seat should be about 450mm above floor level.

A wash basin should be provided inside the compartment. A single lever operated tap is preferable. The basin, toilet flushing handle, paper holder and towel should all be within reach of a person sitting on the toilet.

The location of the toilet should be clearly signposted.

Windows. Windows should be clearly marked.

Floor surfaces and coverings. Plain carpets are preferable for people with low vision. Floor surfaces and coverings should be of a contrasting colour to the skirting boards and walls. Floor surfaces should be slip-resistant, whether wet or dry. Changes in level should be identifiable by lighting or by contrasts in colour of texture. All floor areas should be kept clean and free from any obstruction.

Switches and controls. Light switches should align with door handles. Switches, alarm telephones and controls for lifts, switches and controls for heating installations, ventilation, fire alarms, etc should not be higher than 1400mm above floor level.

Reception and waiting areas and signs. Signplates may be used to identify or advertise the following:

accessible entrances to the building
manageable routes through the building
accessible lifts
accessible toilets
reserved car parking places
the availability of special services in the building.

Signs for direction and location should have large characters or numerals contrasting with the background.

Reception and waiting areas should be clearly signposted from the car park and from the entrance. The areas should also be clearly marked from other rooms inside the building so that clients can find their way back.

Waiting areas should have seating, smoking and non-smoking areas. There should be access to a drinks vending machine.

Induction loops. Induction loops should be installed for the benefit of people with impaired hearing who use certain types of hearing aid.

ASSESSING THE ACCESSIBILITY OF VENUES

Entrance to the building

Is there wheelchair access at the front entrance/at another entrance/at side or back of building?
Are there steps to the front door?
Is there a ramp?
How steep is it?
Is the front entrance door wide enough for a wheelchair?
Is it a revolving door?
Can the door be kept open to let people in?

Inside the building

Doors and corridors – are they wide enough for a wheelchair?
Can a wheelchair pass?
Are there double doors?
Can they be kept open?

Handrails

Are there handrails along the corridors?

Lifts

How many lifts can people with disabilities use (remember people with visual as well as mobility disabilities)?
How wide is the lift?
How far is the walk from the rooms being used?
Does the lift have control buttons at low level?
Does the lift have Braille controls?

The offices and meeting rooms

Are the rooms you are using all on one level?
How far away are they from:
    the reception area?
    other offices?
    refreshment/toilet facilities?

Conference seating

Is there a lecture theatre?
Is the seating moveable?
Is there a raised platform at the front?
Is there a ramp to the platform?

Adapted toilet

How many toilets for people with disabilities are there?
Which floor(s) are they on?
Are they easy to get to/near the lift?
Is there enough room to turn a wheelchair?
Are there handrails and grabrails?
Do the wash basins have adapted taps?
Is there enough space for sideways transfer to the toilets?
Is the chain long enough?
Does it have a metal ring?
Are handtowels/dryers, etc within wheelchair reach?

For people who are deaf or hearing impaired

Is there a loop system in the main room/hall; in other rooms? If not
    can one be fitted?
Is there a microphone in the main room/hall available for other rooms?
Is there a roving microphone?

Refreshment room

Is there a separate room or area?
Will refreshments be served in the meeting room?
Will there be plenty of room for wheelchairs to manoeuvre?

Parking

Is there parking for disabled drivers?
Is there a car park within 100 metres?
How many parking spaces will be available?
Is the ground level from car park to building?
Are there any obstacles?
If road parking, are there yellow lines or other restrictions?
How high is the kerb?

Other transport

How far is the bus stop?
How far is the station?
Is there a taxi service?
Any other means of transport?

Fire procedures
(Check the fire regulations)

Are there procedures for emergency exit?
Are foldable wheelchairs available?
Are available staff and visitors briefed on procedures?
Are emergency situation tasks allocated?
Are there flashing lights as well as bells?

Appendix 4

Useful Names and Addresses

Ability Net
PO Box 94, Warwick,
CV34 5WS
Tel/Min: 01926 312 847
Tel (free): 0800 269545
Web site: www.abilitynet.co.uk

Action for Blind People
14–16 Verney Road, London,
SE16 3DZ
Tel: 020 7732 8771
Fax: 020 7639 0948
Web
site:www.demon.co.uk/afbp

Action for ME
PO Box 1302, Wells, Somerset
Tel: 01749 670799
Web site: www.afme.org.uk

Arthritis Care
18 Stephenson Way, London,
NW1 2HD
Tel/Min 020 7916 1500
Web site:
www.arthritiscare.org.uk

**The Association to Combat
Huntingdon's Chorea**
108 Battersea High Street,
London, SW11 3HP
Tel: 020 7223 7000
Web site: www.had.org.uk

**Association of Disabled
Professionals**
Box BCM ADP, London,
WC1N 3XX
Tel/Fax: 01924 283253
Web site: www.adp.org.uk

**Association for Spina Bifida
and Hydrocephalus (ASBAH)**
ASBAH House, 42 Park Road,
Peterborough, PE1 2UQ
Tel: 01733 555988
Fax: 01733 555985
Web site:
www.asbah.demon.co.uk

**BACUP (British Association
of Cancer United Patients)**
3 Bath Place
Rivington Street
London, EC2A 3JR
Tel/Min: 020 7696 9003
Fax: 020 7696 9002
Web site:
www.cancerbacup.org.uk

Benefit Enquiry Line
Tel: 0800 882200
Min: 0800 243355
(Information on benefits for
disabled people)

Blind in Business
Wingate Annexe, St Alphage
House, 2 Fore Street, London,
EC2Y 5DA
Tel: 020 7588 1885
Fax: 020 7588 1886

Breakthrough
Alangale House, The Close,
Westhill Campus, Bristol Road,
Birmingham, B29 6LN
Tel: 0121 472 6447
Min: 0121 471 1001
Web site:
www.breakthrough/dh1.org.uk

British Colostomy Association
15 Station Road, Reading,
Berkshire, RG1 1LG
Tel: 0118 939 1537
Fax: 0118 956 9095
Web site: www.bcass.org.uk

**British Council of
Organisations of Disabled
People (BCODP)**
Litchurch Plaza, Litchurch Lane,
Derby, DE24 8AA
Tel: 01332 295551
Min: 01332 295581
Web site: www.bcodp.org.uk

**British Deaf Association
(BDA)**
1–3 Worship Street, London,
EC2A 2AB
Tel: 020 7588 3520
Min: 020 7588 3529
Web site: www.bda.org.uk

**British Diabetic Association
(BDA)**
10 Queen Anne Street, London,
W1M 0BD
Tel: 020 7323 1531
Fax: 020 7637 3644
Web site: www.diabetes.org.uk

**British Dyslexia Association
(BDA)**
98 London Road, Reading,
Berkshire, RG1 5AU
Tel: 0118 9668 271
Web site:
www.bda-dyslexia.org.uk

British Epilepsy Association
New Anstey House, Gate Way
Drive, Yeadon, Leeds,
LS19 7XY
Tel: 0113 210 8800
Fax: 0113 391 0300
Helpline: 0808 800 5050
Web site: www.epilepsy.org.uk

British Heart Foundation
14 Fitzharding Street, London,
W1H 4DH
Tel: 020 7935 0185
Fax: 020 7486 5820
Web site: www.bhf.org.uk

**British Limbless
Ex-Servicemen's Association
(BLESMA)**
Frankland Moore House,
185–187 High Road, Chadwell
Heath, Romford, Essex,
RM6 6NA
Tel: 020 8590 1124
E-mail:
www.blesma@btconnect.com

British Polio Fellowship
Ground Floor Unit A, Eagle
Office Centre, The Runway,
South Ruislip, Middlesex,
HA4 6SE
Tel: 020 8842 1898
Freephone: 0800 0180 586
Fax: 020 8842 0555
E-mail:
british.polio@dial.pipex.com

**British Retinitis Pigmentosa
Society**
PO Box 350, Buckingham,
MK18 5EL
Tel: 01280 860 363
Fax: 01280 860 515
Web site:
www.brps.demon.co.uk

**British Sports Association for
the Disabled**
Mary Glen Haig Suite, Solecast
House, 13–27 Brunswick Place,
London, N1 6DX
Tel: 020 7490 4919
Min: 020 7336 8721
Web site: www.euroyellowpages.
com/dse/difpeng/htm

Brittle Bone Society
30 Guthrie Street, Dundee,
DD1 SBF
Tel: 01382 204446
Fax: 01382 206771
Web site:
www.brittlebone.org.uk

CancerLink
11–21 Northdown Street,
London, N1 9BN
Tel/Min: 020 7833 2451

Capability Scotland
22 Corstophine Road,
Edinburgh, EH12 6HP
Tel: 0131 313 5510
Fax: 0131 346 7864
Web site:
www.capability-scotland.org.uk

**Centre for Accessible
Environments**
Nutmeg House, 60 Gainsford
Street, London, SE1 2NY
Tel: 020 7357 8182
Fax: 020 7357 8183
Web site: www.cae.org.uk

Coeliac Society
PO Box 220, High Wycombe,
Bucks, HP11 2HY
Tel: 01494 437 278
Web site: www.coeliac.co.uk

**Community Service Volunteers
(CSV)**
237 Pentonville Road, London,
N1 9NJ
Tel: 020 7278 6601
Fax: 020 7833 0149
Web site: www.csv.org.uk

**Council for the Advancement
of Communication with Deaf
People (CACDP)**
University of Durham, Science
Park, Block 4, Stockton Road,
Durham, DH1 3UZ
Tel/Min: 0191 383 1155
Minicom ansaphone:
0191 383 7915
Web site:
www.cacdp.demon.co.uk

Cystic Fibrosis Trust
11 London Road, Bromley,
Kent, BR1 1BY
Tel: 020 8464 7211
Fax: 020 8313 0472
Web site: www.cftrust.org.uk

DIAL UK (National Association of Disablement Information and Advice Lines)
Park Lodge, St Catherine's
Hospital, Tickhill Road,
Doncaster, DN4 8QN
Tel/Min: 01302 310 123
Web site:
www.members@aol.com/dialuk

The Disabilities Trust
32 Market Place, Burgess Hill,
West Sussex, RH15 9NP
Tel: 01444 239 123
Web site:
www.disabilities-trust.org.uk

Disability Action (Northern Ireland)
2 Annadale Avenue, Belfast,
BT7 3JH
Tel: 028 9049 1011
Min: 028 9064 5779
Web site:
www.disabilityaction.org.uk

Disability Alliance (DA)
Universal House, 88–94
Wentworth Street, London,
E1 7SA
Tel: 020 7247 8776
Rights line Tel/Min:
020 7247 8763

Disability Law Service
39–45 Cavell Street, London,
E1 2BP
Tel: 020 7791 9800
Fax: 020 7831 5582

Disability Rights Commission
London Office, 7th Floor,
226 Gray's Inn Road,
London, WC1X 8HL
Public enquiries: 020 7925 5555
(See 'DRC Information' below)

Disability Scotland
Princes House, 5 Shandwick
Place, Edinburgh, EH2 4RG
Tel/Min: 0131 229 8632
Web site:
www.disabilityscotland.org.uk

Disability Wales
'Llys Ifor', Crescent Road,
Mid Glamorgan, CF83 1XL
Tel/Min: 029 2088 7325

Disability West Midlands
Prospect Hall, College Walk,
Selly Oak, Birmingham,
B29 6LE
Tel: 0121 414 1616
Min: 0121 414 1188
E-mail: disabilitywm@
netscapeonline.co.uk

Disabled Living Foundation (DLF)
380–384 Harrow Road,
London, W9 2HU
Tel: 020 7289 6111
Fax: 020 7266 2922
Web site: www.dlf.org.uk

Disablement Income Group (DIG)
PO Box 5743, Finchingfield,
CM7 4PW
Tel: 01371 811 621

Diversity UK
3 Abbey Square, Turvey,
Bedford, MK43 8DJ
Tel: 01234 811 380
Web site:www.diversityuk.co.uk

Down's Syndrome Association
155 Mitcham Road, London,
SW17 9PG
Tel: 020 8682 4001
Fax: 020 8682 4012
Web site:
www.downs-syndrome.org.uk

DRC Information
Freepost, MIDO 2164,
Stratford on Avon, CV37 9BR
Tel: 08457 622 633
Web site: www.disability.gov.uk
E-mail: enquiries@drc/gb.org

Driver & Vehicle Licensing Agency
Information Branch, Long View
Road, Swansea, SA9 7JL
Tel: 01792 782 341
Web site:
www.open.gov.uk/dvla/dvla.htm

Dyslexia Institute
133 Gresham Road, Staines,
Middlesex, TW18 2AJ
Tel: 01784 463 851
Fax: 01784 460 747
Web site:
www.dyslexia-1nst.org.uk

Employers Forum on Disability
Nutmeg House, 60 Gainsford
Street, London, SE1 2NY
Tel/Min: 020 7403 3020

Federation of Multiple Sclerosis Therapy Centres
Beds & Northants MS Therapy
Centre, Bradbury House,
155 Barkers Lane, Bedford,
MK14 9RX
Tel: 01234 325 781
Fax: 01234 365 242

Greater London Advice on Disability (GLAD)
336 Brixton Road, London,
SW97AA
Tel: 020 7346 5800
Min: 020 7346 5811

Haemophilia Society
Chesterfield House, 385 Euston
Road, London, NW1 3AU
Tel: 020 7380 0600
Fax: 020 7387 8220
Web site:
www.haemophilia.org.uk

Headway – National Head Injuries Association
4 King Edward Court, King
Edward Street, Nottingham,
NG1 1EW
Tel: 0115 924 0800
Fax: 0115 924 0432
Web site: www.headway.org.uk

Hearing Concern
7–11 Armstrong Road, London,
W3 7JL
Tel: 020 8743 1110
Min: 020 8742 9151
Web site: www.
ukonline.co.uk/hearing.concern/

Ileostomy Association of GB and Eire
PO Box 132, Scunthorpe,
DN15 9YW
Tel: 01724 720 150
Fax: 01724 721 601
Web site: www.
ileostomypouch.demon.co.uk

LEAD Scotland (Linking Education and Disability)
Queen Margaret University
College, Clerwood Terrace,
Edinburgh, EH12 8TS
Tel: 0131 317 3439
Fax: 0131 339 7198
Web site: www.lead.org.uk

Leukaemia Care Society
14 Kingfisher Court, Venny
Bridge, Pinhoe, Exeter, Devon,
EX4 8JN
Tel: 01392 464 848
Web site:
www.leukaemiacare.org.uk

MENCAP
123 Golden Lane, London,
EC1Y 0RT
Tel: 020 7454 0454
Fax: 020 7608 3254
Web site: www.mencap.org.uk

Mental Health Foundation
20–21 Cornwall Terrace
London, NW1 4QL
Tel: 020 7535 7400
Fax: 020 7535 7474
Web site:
www.mentalhealth.org.uk

MIND National Association for Mental Health
Granta House, 15–19 Broadway,
Stratford, London, E15 4BQ
Tel: 020 7519 2122
Fax: 020 8522 1725
Web site: www.mind.org.uk

Mobility Advice & Vehicle Information Service (MAVIS)
'O' Wing, Macadam Avenue,
Old Wokingham Road,
Crowthorne, Berks, RG45 6XD
Tel: 01344 661 000
Web site:
www.mobility.unit.detr.gov.uk

Motability
Goodman House, Station
Approach, Harlow, Essex,
CM20, 2ET
Tel: 01279 635 666
Web site: www.motability.co.uk

Multiple Sclerosis Society of Great Britain and Northern Ireland
25 Effie Road, Fulham, London,
SW6 1EE
Tel: 020 7610 7171
Fax: 020 7736 9861
Web site: www.mssociety.org.uk

Muscular Dystrophy Group of Great Britain and Northern Ireland
7–11 Prescott Place, London,
SW4 6BS
Tel: 020 7720 8055
Fax: 020 7498 0670
Web site:
www.muscular-dystrophy.org.uk

Myalgic Encephalomyelitis (ME) Association
4 Corringham Road, Stanford le Hope, Essex, SS17 0AH
Tel: 01375 642 466
Fax: 01375 360 256
Web site: www.meassociation.org.uk

National Asthma Campaign (NAC)
Providence House, Providence Place, London, N1 0NT
Tel: 020 7226 2260
Fax: 020 7704 0740
Web site: www.asthma.org.uk

National Autistic Society
393 City Road, London, EC1V 1NA
Tel: 020 7833 2299
Fax: 020 7833 9666
Web site: www.oneworld.org/autism-uk/

National Backpain Association
16 Elm Tree Road, Teddington, Middlesex, TW11 8ST
Tel: 020 8977 5474
Fax: 020 8943 5318
Web site: www.backpain.org.uk

National Deaf Childrens Society (NDCS)
15 Dufferin Street, London, EC1Y 8UR
Tel/Min: 020 7250 0123
Web site: www.ndcs.org.uk

National Deaf-Blind and Rubella Association (SENSE)
11–13 Clifton Terrace, Finsbury Park, London, N4 3SR
Tel: 020 7272 7774
Min: 020 7272 9648
Web site: www.sense.org.uk

National Eczema Society (NES)
163, Eversholt Street, London, NW1 1BU
Tel: 020 7388 4097
Fax: 020 7388 5882
Web site: www.eczema.org.uk

National Federation of the Blind (NFB)
The Old Surgery
215 Kirkgate, Wakefield, WF1 1JG
Tel: 01924 291 313
Fax: 01924 200 244
Web site: www.
users.globalnet.co.uk/@NFBUK

National Music and Disability Information Service (Sound Sense)
Riverside House, Rattlesden, Bury St Edmunds, IP30 0SF
Tel: 01449 736 287
Web site: www.thenortheast.com/ss

National Schizophrenia Fellowship (NSF)
28 Castle Street, Kingston-upon-Thames, Surrey, KT1 1SS
Tel: 020 8547 3937
Fax: 020 8547 3862
Web site: www.nsf.org.uk

National Society for Epilepsy
Chalfont Centre for Epilepsy, Chesham Lane, Chalfont St Peter, Bucks, SL9 0RJ
Tel: 01494 601 300
Helpline: 01494 601 400
Web site: www.epilepsynse.org.uk

209

Parkinson's Disease Society
215 Foxhill Bridge Road,
London, SW1V 1EL
Tel: 020 7931 8080
E-mail:
mailbox@pdsnk.demon.co.uk

Partially Sighted Society
Queens Road, Doncaster,
DN1 2NX
Tel: 01302 323 132
Fax: 01302 368 998

People First
Instrument House, 207–215
Kings Cross Road, London,
WC1X 9DB
Tel: 020 7713 6400
Fax: 020 7833 1880

Queen Elizabeth's Foundation for Disabled People
Banstead Place Mobility Centre,
Damsen Way, Fountain Drive,
Carshalton, Surrey, SM5 4NR
Tel: 020 8770 1151
E-mail: mobility@
banstead.53.freeserve.co.uk

RADAR (Royal Association for Disability and Rehabilitation)
12 City Forum, 250 City Road,
London, EC1V 8AF
Tel: 020 7250 3222
Min: 020 7250 4119
Web site: www.radar.org.uk

Rathbone CI
Fourth Floor, Churchgate House,
56 Oxford Street, Manchester,
M1 6EU
Tel: 0161 236 5358
Fax: 0161 236 4539
Web site: www.rathboneci-demon.co.uk

Regards
Unit 2J, Leeroy House, 436
Essex Road, London, N1 3QP
Tel: 020 7688 4111
Web site:
www.regard.dircon.co.uk

Remploy Limited
415 Edgware Road,
Cricklewood, London,
NW2 6LR
Tel: 020 8235 0535

Repetitive Strain Injury (RSI) Association
380–384 Harrow Road, London,
W9 2HU
Tel: 020 7266 2000
Fax: 020 7266 4114

Restricted Growth Association
PO Box 8, Countesthorpe,
Leicester, LE8 525
Tel/Fax: 0116 247 8913
Web site: www.rga1talk21.com

Royal National Institute for the Blind (RNIB)
224 Great Portland Street,
London, W1N 6AA
Tel: 020 7388 1266
Fax: 020 7388 2034
Web site: www.rnib.org.uk

Royal National Institute for Deaf People (RNID)
19–23 Featherstone Street,
London, EC1Y 8SL
Tel: 020 7296 8000
Min: 020 7296 8001
Web site: www.rnid.org.uk

Scope
6 Market Road, London,
N7 9PW
Tel: 020 7619 7222
Fax: 020 7619 7399
Web site: www.scope.org.uk
Cerebral Palsy Helpline:
0800 3333

Shaw Trust
Shaw House, Epsom Square,
White Horse Business Park,
Trowbridge, Wiltshire,
BA14 0XJ
Tel: 01225 716 350
Min: 0345 697 288
Fax: 01225 716 334

Sickle Cell Society
54 Station Road, London,
NW10 4UA
Tel: 020 8961 7795
Fax: 020 8961 8346
Web site:
www.sicklecellsociety.org.uk

Skill: National Bureau for Students with Disabilities
Chapter House, 18–20 Crucifix
Lane, London, SE1 3JW
Tel/Min: 020 7450 0620
Information Service:
0800 328 5050 (Tel)
0800 068 2422 (Text)
Web site: www.skill.org.uk

Spinal Injuries Association (SIA)
76 St James' Lane, London,
N10 3DF
Tel: 020 8444 2121
Fax: 020 8444 3761
Web site: www.spinal.co.uk

SPOD
286 Camden Road, London,
N7 0BJ
Tel: 020 7607 8851/2

Stammering Association
15 Old Ford Road, London,
E2 9PJ
Tel: 020 8983 1003
Fax: 020 8983 3591
Web site:
www.stammering.org.uk

Stroke Association
Stroke House, Whitecross Street,
London, EC1Y 8JJ
Tel: 020 7490 7999
Fax: 020 7490 2686
Web site: www.stroke.org.uk

Terrence Higgins Trust
52–54 Gray's Inn Road,
London, WC1X 8JU
Tel: 0171 831 0330
Helpline: 020 7242 1010
Fax: 020 7242 0121
Web site: www.tht.org.uk

Values into Action
Oxford House, Derbyshire
Street, London, W4 5JL
Tel: 020 7729 5436
Fax: 020 7729 0436
Web site: www.demon.co.uk\via

Workable (Employment for Disabled People)
3rd Floor, 67–71 Goswell Road,
London, EC1V 7EP
Tel/Min: 020 7608 3161
Web site: www.members.
aol.com/workableuk\index.htm

LOCAL EMPLOYER NETWORKS ON DISABILITY

Birmingham
Rosemary Martin, Coordinator, Birmingham Employers' Network on Disability, c/o Cadbury Ltd, 83 Bournville Lane, Birmingham, B30 2HP
Tel: 0121 451 2227
Web site: www.bitc.org.uk

Calderdale and Kirklees
Karen Merron/Siraj Mayet, Employers' Network, Waverly House, Huddersfield, West Yorkshire, HD1 5NA
Tel: 01484 426256

Fife
Duncan Reid, Fife Employers' Network on Disability, Commerce House, 17 Tolbooth Street, Kirkcaldy, Fife, KY1 1RW
Tel: 01592 201932

Hampshire
Ron Whitehouse, Hampshire Employers' Network on Disability, Manor Hatch, 63 Southampton Road, Ringwood, Hampshire, BH24 1HE
Tel: 01703 555655

Milton Keynes and North Bucks
Lesley Taylor, Coordinator, Milton Keynes and North Bucks Disability Employment Network, c/o VAG (UK) Ltd, Yeomans Drive, Blakelands, Milton Keynes, MK14 5AN
Tel: 01908 601349

Northern Ireland
Cecil Porter, Development Officer, Northern Ireland Employers' Forum on Disability, Business in the Community, c/o BP Oil UK Ltd, Retail Field Office, Airport Road West, Belfast, BT3 9EA
Tel: 01232 739639

Thames Valley
TVENOD, Connaught House, 365 Oxford Road, Reading, RG30 1HA
Tel: 0118 958 8083

Your DEA should have news of local initiatives if the above do not apply to you.

Bibliography

Austin Knight UK Ltd (1996) *Equality at Work*, Austin Knight, London.

BIFU (1992) *Breaking down Barriers*, BIFU, London.

BIFU (1987) *Opening Doors*, BIFU, London.

Bosley, S (1994) *Able to Succeed: Disabilities, health and job choice*, Cascaid, Leicester.

Brading, J (1996) *New Perspectives: A handbook for careers staff working with students and graduates with disabilities*, Skill, London.

Clutterbuck, D and Snow, D (1990) *Working with the Community: A guide to corporate social responsibility*, Weidenfeld, London.

Cox, T (1992) 'Can equal opportunities be made more equal?', *Harvard Business Review*, March–April, 1, 142.

Department for Education and Employment (1999) *Employing Disabled People: A good practice guide for employers and managers*, DfEE, London (obtainable free from DRC Information – see Appendix 4).

Department for Education and Employment (1999) *From Exclusion to Inclusion*, a report by the Disability Rights Task Force on civil rights for disabled people, DfEE, London.

Disability Information Trust (1994) *Employment and the Workplace*, DIT, Oxford.

Diversity UK (1999) *The Diversity Directory*, Diversity UK, Bedford.

Doyle, B J (1996) *Disability Discrimination: Law and practice*, Jordans, Bristol.

Employers' Forum on Disability (1994) Disability Action File, EFD, London.

Employment Service (1994) *Becoming a Disability Symbol User*, ES, Sheffield.

English Heritage (1995) *Easy Access to Historic Properties*, English Heritage, London.

Gooding, C (1996) *Blackstone's Guide to the Disability Discrimination Act 1995*, Blackstone, London.

GPMU (formerly SOGAT) (undated) *Workers with Disabilities: Taking away the obstacles*, Bedford.

Honey, S, Meager, N and Williams, M (1993) *Employers' Attitudes Towards People with Disabilities*, Institute of Manpower (now Employment) Studies, Brighton.

Kandola, R and Fullerton, J (1994) *Managing the Mosaic: Diversity in action*, IPD, London.

Kettle, M (1979) *Disabled People and their Employment*, Association of Disabled Professionals, London.

McEnroe, M P (1993) 'Managing diversity' *Organisational Dynamics*, Winter, 21, 3, 18–29.

Meager, N et al (1999) *Monitoring the DDA*, IES, Brighton.

Milton Keynes and North Bucks Disability Employment Network (1996) *Disability Action File*, Milton Keynes.

NALGO: *More Than Ramps*, NALGO, London.

OCR (1999) *Access to Vocational Assessment*, OCR, Coventry.

Office for National Statistics (1999) *Labour Market Trends, September 1999*, Office for National Statistics, London.

Prescott-Clarke, P (1990) *Employment and Handicap*, SCPR, London.

RNIB (1999) *The Get Back! Pack: Adapting to change when an employee becomes disabled*, RNIB, Peterborough.

SHL (1993) *Guidelines for Best Practice in the Use of Assessment and Development Centres*, SHL, Thames Ditton.

SHL (1993) *Guidelines for Testing People with Disabilities*, SHL, Thames Ditton.

The Stationery Office (1994) *Disability Rights Commission Act 1999*, The Stationery Office, Norwich.

The Stationery Office (1995) *Disability Discrimination Act 1995*, The Stationery Office, Norwich.

The Stationery Office (1996) *Code of Practice for the Elimination of Discrimination in the Field of Employment against Disabled Persons or Persons who have had a Disability*, The Stationery Office, Norwich.

The Stationery Office (1996) *Guidance on Matters to be Taken Into Account in Determining Questions Relating to the Definition of Disability*, The Stationery Office, Norwich.

The Stationery Office (1999) *Code of Practice: Duties of trade organizations to their disabled members and applicants*, The Stationery Office, Norwich.

The Stationery Office (1999) *Code of Practice: Rights of access – goods, facilities, services and premises*, The Stationery Office, Norwich.

Thomas, A (1992) *Working with a Disability: Barriers and facilitators*, SCPR, London.

TUC (1985, 1989) *TUC Guide on the Employment of Disabled People*, TUC, London.

Index

access
  assessment 200–202
  external and internal building
    specifications 196–200
  wheelchairs 39, 67
  see also workplace
Access to Work 110–11
action *see* practices
action groups 37
addiction 124
Advisory Conciliation and
  Arbitration Service
  (ACAS) 96
age 22
AIDS/HIV 156
alcohol 124
allergies 125
apprenticeships 114–15
arthritis 156
assessment and development
  centres (AC/DC) 65–66
asthma 25, 132–33, 156
Austin Knight Ltd
  Equality at Work survey 58
autism 156

back injury 27
Blind in Business 113

body piercing, non-medical
  125
Bosley, S 25
brittle bones 25, 157
Brown, Paul 131
Business and Technology
  Education Council 116

cancer 157
career development 73–74
  policies 91
cerebral palsy 157
City and Guilds 116
Clark v *Novacold* 137
*Code of Practice – Duties of
  Trade Organisations*
  (The Stationery Office)
  141
*Code of Practice: Rights of
  access – goods, facilities,
  services and premises*
  (The Stationery Office)
  150
*Code of Practice for the
  Elimination of
  Discrimination*
  (The Stationery Office)
  88, 122, 135

Code of Practice on Employment (The Stationery Office) 53
Code of Practice on the Employment of Disabled People (The Stationery Office) 88–90
coeliac syndrome 157
colostomy 157
communication
  co-ordination with disabled employees 89–90
  identifying the barriers 41–42
community 91
comparators 137
Compliance Cost Assessment (DfEE) 84
continence 126, 127
contract workers 140
Coverdale Organisation 39
Cox, T 36–37
Cox v *The Post Office* 132–33
curriculum vitae 60–61
customers 34, 37
cystic fibrosis 157

deafness and hearing impairment
  access 67–68
  assessing access 201
  employer policies 39
  substantial effects 126, 127–28
  workplace implications 28
Dearing Report 116, 117
diabetes 157
disability
  behaviour and environment 125–26
  cumulative effects 125
  defining 24–26, 122–28
  distinction between impairment, disability and handicap 25
  duration 128
  effects of treatment 126
  exclusions from definition 124–25
  implication of types for workplace 26–31
  issues raised by gene technology 155
  medical, tragedy and social models 42–43
  some common conditions 156–60
  substantial effects 125–28
  versus inabilities 16
Disability Discrimination: Law and practice (Doyle) 129–30
Disability Discrimination Act (1995)
  defining disability 25–26, 122–28
  dismissal 131–33
  education 150–51
  employment provisions 121–22
  likely impact 147–48
  provisions of 13–14, 15–16, 96–97
  regulations for all services and premises 149–50
  summary 119–20
  trade unions 140–41
  transport 152
  who is affected 12
The Disability Discrimination (Employment) Regulations 1996 122, 138–40
The Disability Discrimination (Meaning of Disability) Regulations 122
disability employment advisors (DEAs) 109

Disability Now (Scope newspaper) 58
Disability Rights Commission 13–14
provision for 119–20
Disability Rights Commission Act 1999 97
provisions of 152–53
see also complete Statute in Appendix 2
Disability Rights Task Force 153–54
selection tests 65
Disability Service 113
teams 109
disability symbol 59
five commitments 112–13
disabled people
case for employment 32–33
current employment statistics 23
as customers 34
effect of Disability Discrimination Act 1995 on 12
involvement in policy 91
specialist services for 109
tips on tact and etiquette 49
Disabled Persons (Employment) Act 1944 15, 122
discrimination 129–30
defining 130
disfigurement 126
dismissal
and earlier legislation 130–33
fair reasons for 130–31
justification 134
provisions of the Disability Discrimination Act 1995 15
disputes and complaints 141–42
questionnaire procedure 142–46

diversity
personal competence 50
trainers 45
valuing 36–37
Diversity Directory 45
Down's syndrome 157–58
Doyle, B J 129–30, 134
drugs 124
Du Pont survey 33
dyslexia 28
case study 64

educational institutions
as a provider of goods, facilities and services 151
as employers 150
disability statements 151
effect of The Disability Discrimination Act 1995 on 12, 13
Open University Code of Practice 95–106
qualification for disabled people 23
Egan, Gerard 47
employees
becoming disabled while employed 75–78, 82
career development 73–74
continuing support 102–03
current trends 21–22
demographic changes 22
dismissal 80–82
diversity 34–37
redundancy 78–79
resistance to promoting good practice 46–47
terms and conditions of service 69–70
types of disabilities 26–31
welcoming and supporting new recruits 70–71

work experience 38, 85–86, 103
see also pay, benefits and pensions; recruitment
Employers' Attitudes Towards People with Disabilities (IES) 26
Employers' Forum on Disability 114
aims and agenda 90–91
Monitoring Disability in the Workplace 39
Welcoming Disabled Customers 34
employers/organizations
case for employing disabled people 32–36
corporate social responsibility 33–43
costs 84–85
discrimination 129–30
duty to make reasonable adjustments 134–37
educational establishments 150
effect of the Disability Discrimination Act 1995 12
Midland Bank's disability policy 37–40
monitoring performance 87, 91
motivation towards improvements 31–32
previous inactivity 16–17
provisions of Act 13, 15–16, 121–22
publicizing policy statements 93
seeking outside advice 86
specialist services support 109–10

suggested objectives 89
support networks 114
Employment and Handicap Survey (Prescott-Clarke) 108
Employment Appeal Tribunal (EAT) 124
Employment Tribunals Service 141
enforcement
Disability Rights Commission 152–53
monitoring 105
epilepsy 25, 157
case study 79–80
workplace implications 31
equal opportunities
Midland Bank's policy statement 92–93
policies 90
valuing diversity 34–36
Equality at Work (Austin Knight survey) 58
ethnic minorities
demographic changes 22
exhibitionism 125

Fozard v *Greater Manchester Police Authority* 54
Fullerton, J 35
funding
workplace adjustments 135
Further and Higher Education Act 1992 151

GCSEs and A Levels 115–16
gene technology 154
General National Vocational Qualifications (GNVQs) 115–16
Get Back (RNIB) 82
Goodwin v *The Patent Office* 124, 125

government
plans for action 88–90
Guidance on Matters to be Taken Into Account (The Stationery Office) 128

haemophilia 158
Hardy v *Gower Furniture Ltd* 81, 137
health and safety 79–80
consciousness 33
policies 104–05
heart disease 158
Henley Management College 22
HIV/AIDS 155
Honey, S 16, 84
Howden v *Capital Copiers (Edinburgh) Ltd* 74–75, 133

Institute of Employment Studies 31–32
Employers' Attitudes Towards People with Disabilities 26
insurance 83–84
intellectual tasks 126, 127
interviews, recruitment 57, 68–69, 101–02
Investors in People 95

Job Introduction Scheme (JIS) 111–12

Kandola, R 35
Kenny v *Hampshire Constabulary* 136
Kettle, M 16
Kirker v *British Sugar plc* 78–79, 131

Labour Relations Agency (LRA) 96

Lang v *Redland Roofings Systems Ltd* 29–30
language
preferred expressions 48–49
Learning and Skills Councils 117
learning difficulties
dyslexia 28
workplace implications 28

management
continuing professional development 95
disability awareness training 43–46
motivation for improvements 33
personal skills for diversity competence 50
proactive programmes 82
training for disability equality 38
valuing diversity 34–37
Massie, Bert 120, 153
Matty v *Tesco Stores Ltd* 55–56
McEnroe, M P 50
ME (myalgic encephalomyelitis) 123, 157–58
medical opinion 16–17
Mencap 113
mental health 159
workplace implications 29–30
Midland Bank plc
disability policy 37–40
Equal Opportunities Policy 92–94
Modern Apprenticeships and People with Disabilities 115
monitoring
infringment of code of practice 105

Monitoring Disability in the Workplace (Employers' Forum) 39
Morse v *Wiltshire County Council* 136, 138
multiple sclerosis 159
Murphy v *Sheffield Hallam University* 129
muscular dystrophy 159
myalgic encephalomyelitis (ME) 123, 158–59

National Disability Council 152
provisions of Act 13–14
National Record of Achievement (NRA) 116–17
National Vocational Qualifications (NVQs) 115–16
career development 73–74
New Deal 117
nicotine addiction 124
Northern Ireland
provisions of the Disability Discrimination Act 1995 14

O'Dea v *Bonart Ltd* 74
O'Neill v *Symm & Co Ltd* 123
Open University
Code of Good Practice 95–106
organizations *see* employers/organizations

pay, benefits and pensions
employer policies 38
provision in Act 138–40
sickness absence 73–75
People Management (journal) 132

physical and mobility impairments
access 67
substantial effects 126, 127
traumatic injuries 159
workplace implications 26–27
policy and practice
employer co-ordination with disabled employees 89–90
Employers' Forum 90–91
government suggestions 88–90
Midland Bank 92–94
model statement 94
Open University 95–106
organization-specific codes 92–93
political correctness 48
practice *see* policy and practice
Prescott-Clarke, P
Employment and Handicap Survey 108
property owners
effect of Disability Discrimination Act 1995 12, 13
psychometric testing 62–65
psychoses 159
pyromania 124

recruitment
advertising 57–58, 99
applications/CVs 60–61
assessment and development centres 65–66
attracting people with disabilities 59–60, 112–13
discrimination 129

interviews   57, 68–69, 101–02
job descriptions   53–54,
    98–99
Open University Code of
    Good Practice   98–102
personal specifications
    55–56, 98–99
policies   91
present practices   60
psychometric testing   62–65
reasonable workplace
    adjustments   52–53
selection techniques   57
shortlisting candidates
    100–01
redundancy   78–79, 137–38
rehabilitation   103–04
counselling   82
employer policies   38
repetitive strain injury (RSI)
    159
resistance to good practice
    46–47
retention
policies   91
rehabilitation   103–04
supporting newly disabled
    employees   75–8, 82
rheumatism   159
rheumatoid arthritis   158
Roffey Park Management
    Institute   32
Rowley v *Walkers Nonsuch Ltd*
    27
Royal Association for Disability
    and Rehabilitation   114
Royal National Institute for the
    Blind   113

Samuels v *Wesleyan Assurance*
    Society   81–82
Sandy v *Hampshire*
    Constabulary   70

Saville and Holdsworth UK Ltd
    63, 66
schizophrenia   159–60
Scope   113
self-employment   22, 23
service providers   12
sexual abuse   125
Seymour v *British Airways*
    Board   131
sickle cell anaemia   160
sickness absence   73–75
Smith v *Carpets International*
    UK plc   79–80
speech and language
    impairments
substantial   126, 127
workplace implications
    30
spina bifida   160
sponsorship   39–40
stress   22
stroke   159
support
apprenticeship and
    qualifications schemes
    114–18
categories   108
employer networks   114
funding   110–11
statutory help   109–13
voluntary sector   113–14
Supported Employment
    Programme   111

tact
meeting disabled people
    49
preferred language   48–49
Tarling v *Wisdom Toothbrushes*
    Ltd   147–8
tattoos   125
teleworking
current trends   22

testing
  psychometric   63–65
  recruitment selection
      techniques   57
theft   125
Thomas, A   16–17
Thompson, Sir Peter   22
trade unions
  provisions of Disability
      Discrimination Act 1995
      140–41
training
  apprenticeship and
      qualifications schemes
      114–18
  disability awareness   43–46,
      90–91
  disability equality for
      management   38
  employee career development
      73–74
  organizing and designing
      44–45
  policies   90–91
  provisions of the Disability
      Discrimination Act 1995
      15
  qualification schemes and
      initiatives   115–18
  retraining newly disabled
      employees   76–77, 91
  work experience   38, 85–86,
      103
Training and Enterprise
    Councils (TECs)   117
transport
  provisions of Act   152

unemployment
  current statistics   23

victimization   147
visual impairment
  access   68
  employer policies   38
  substantial effects   126, 127–8
  workplace implications   27
voyeurism   125

Welcoming Disabled Customers
    (Employers' Forum)   34
wheelchairs   39, 67 *see also*
    access
Williams v *Channel 5*
    Engineering Services Ltd
    53
women
  demographic changes   22
Wood v *Darron Motors Ltd*
    76
Workable   113
workplace
  access   67–68, 104
  Access to Work remove
      obstacles   110–11
  current trends   21–22
  duty of employer to make
      changes   134–37
  health and safety   79–80
  physical features   138
  policies   91
  reasonable adjustments
      52–53
  regulations for all services
      and premises
      149–50
  special equipment/
      adaptations   39
  substantial effects of
      environment   125–26
  testing arrangements   64